GOD
IS IN
YOUR
MESS

CINDY SCHMIDLER

FUSION
HYBRID PUBLISHING

Library of Congress Control Number: 2023920032
Paperback ISBN: 9781637971765
Hardback ISBN: 9781637971758
eBook ISBN: 9781637971772

Cover by Dan Pitts
Interior Design by Typewriter Creative Co.

Printed in the United States of America
10 9 8 7 6 5 4 3 2 1

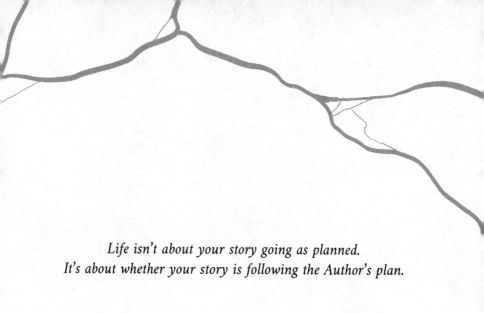

Life isn't about your story going as planned.
It's about whether your story is following the Author's plan.

CONTENTS

INTRODUCTION

God shut the door on Noah's ark at just the precise time. He sealed Noah and his family in. In the same way, we are hemmed in, before and behind. We are knitted in our mother's womb until just the right moment. As God said,

Your day today has been written in God's book even before your life began (Psalm 139:16, my paraphrase).

What if we felt as secure as that? Sealed in our Father's care like Noah and his family, safe as when in our mother's womb with not a care in the world? What if we placed God in the middle of our every situation, good and bad? What if we could know His truth in such a way as to believe He is right in it with us and has us on all sides? More than a mere human parent cheerleading for her child or a stadium of fans excitedly waiting for someone to come on stage? Cheering for us not only when we are winning or when we are exceeding in life, but times when we've been left off the roster? Times when we've been abandoned and no one considers us of any importance.

What then? What if in our lonely seasons we believed God promises an A-plus, over the top result? What if we believed in God's utmost care when we feel shattered and laid out bare?

What then? We would have to close the book. We'd have to start thriving. We'd have to begin joyfully living in our God-given abundance right in the middle of our pain.

As Psalm 23:6 (my paraphrase) concludes, "Surely goodness and mercy shall follow me all the days of my life and then I will go home and dwell happily with the Lord."

Happy here, happy ever after; win-win.

But I'm confident that you are like me. Some days are like pulling teeth. Getting out of bed is hard.

I often pray, "I believe you, Lord, that You do care for me and my troubles, but maybe just not today. Lord, I need You to bring my whole being, my emotions, passions, desires, thoughts, affections, my less than confident trust, to a relentless certainty. I need to know that You've got me this day. Please, God."

Well, we can know. He wrote a whole book of certain, authentic, legitimate, and undeniable stories that can lead us to a stable and unshakable foundation of trust in Him.

So come with me. Please bring your shovel, because together we are going to dig into a place where irresistible treasures lie, hope reigns, and abundance flourishes. We will dare to ask for the secret to eternal happiness and find the place where God proposes our desires and our thoughts to live. A 24/7 place of life-giving, milk and honey life. A place where skies are clear and the sun shines brightly. A refreshing place of perpetual holiday at sea where all days are smooth sailing and rejoicing is the main event.

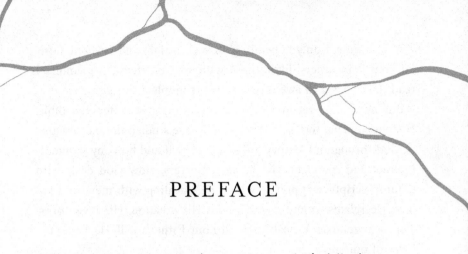

PREFACE

HE'S planned it, therefore it's marvelous and it's full of purpose. Those are words to abundant life.

This book was written to shine a beacon of light into our dark tunnels.

It was written to reveal our defective lenses.

We eat leftover scraps saved for dogs when a King's fare of His richest delicacies await us with succulent choices of the finest of foods for our souls. Come see how we refine our palates.

This book was written to reveal how God causes ALL things so marvelously! If we could see it now, our hearts would burst!

I've written to bring confidence and security to our anxious lives.

I've written so we can have assurance in God's specific and supreme plan for each one of us.

I've written to reveal a crystal-clear view of God's wisdom so we can see Him working in the deep and dark parts of our lives, the tunnels where our navigation is lost.

God's Supremacy

As I have searched and studied God's supremacy, I've been overwhelmed with His super colossal highness. Nothing in all eternity seems to come near. What I've come to understand has offered me a rock-solid confidence. The cement I needed to trust Him more fully and have the ability to see His commanding presence in my life.

At one time, I only hoped to gain such insight and wisdom. Sure, I'd seen it in others' lives, those with sold out faith in memoirs I read that left me in awe of what they triumphed through.

But now, after reading God's outstanding love letter, the Bible, His phenomenal instruction manual, I have studied these characters of God throughout history. I now see myself and how my moments interact and correlate with these characters. How God deals with them in scripture is precisely how He's dealing with me also. I see how He relates to and engages with His creation, His loved ones. This is a wonderful sneak peek into our Father's will. He, being the lover of our souls.

Paul prayed for the people in Colossians 1:9 (my paraphrase): *"God, pour out your Holy Spirit upon us. Remove our dimness, the blind pieces that keep us from seeing who you really are."*

By the time you finish reading, I'm confident and quite certain, as was true for me, you will gain wisdom and confidence to advance in whatever ascent God has commissioned for you.

I'm thinking of nail-biting, paralyzing, heart-pumping projects He calls us to. His purposes are always outside our comfort zones, aren't they? We must seek His help and let Him head our plans. Just like Moses said to God, *"don't send me. I'm not qualified to speak for you, Lord"* (Exodus 4:10, my paraphrase).

That is the exact point in which we are ready.

It's through the fiercest storm we need the firm foundation of God's promising truth, truth to anchor our souls to and truth that places God in the center of our every circumstance. Truth our hearts desperately need to thrive.

How God Holds Us

Imagine this. What if you knew someone who loved you so much that they always did the very best for you? Their eyes completely focused on you alone. They cared for you and protected you supernaturally. They never slept. They stood in constant watch over you. How would you feel?

You'd probably feel like me—kept, light, free, happy, bold, brave, calm, composed, confident, cool, with not a single care in the world, right? Well, this is how God holds us.

Come see through these pages how true it all is.

God's goal is for you and I to know Him completely.

So buckle up, get the coffee you've been dreaming about, and let the words of our God unfold over your soul. Allow them to nourish and strengthen you. These words declare Who our supreme, heavenly Father is to us.

The Story of John

The story of John, not John the Baptist nor John the Apostle, but John THE SCHMIDLER.

"Honey, are you sure about this? You have never worked in education."

Since his Portuguese man o'war sting, John's had been all guns blazing when it came to new adventures. Was that his brush with death? But that's a story for another sit-down.

After his significantly emotional event in the Caribbean, John took some time off to explore what God might call him to. He had already left his large corporate job of twenty-plus years, an apprehensive decision that turned out to be a perfectly planned work of God.

Hindsight is so reassuring, isn't it? And yet it often feels too late.

One of the opportunities presented to John was the ability to turn around a Christian college. The college was hemorrhaging; no tourniquet could stop the bleeding. It was on life support. Someone needed to come and resurrect the balance sheet.

John came running into the house.

Startled, I asked him, "Honey, how much coffee did you drink at that breakfast meeting?"

I was sure he had been mainlining expresso or something. He could not contain his excitement.

"Cindy, this project is a thrill of a lifetime. You know me, the direr the balance sheet, the more intoxicating." For John, it was a challenging puzzle of the double dare kind he thrives on. The chance to make a difference was invigorating to him.

But perhaps it would be best to see how the whole process worked, step by step. And in it, see how God was directing the whole thing.

John's Initial Meeting

"Joe, great to see you," John warmly greeted a friend he hadn't seen in a long time. They chitchatted guy style. Work, business, and world affairs while waiting for a table to open up at John's favorite lunch haunt, Bravos.

Joe was meeting an employee and John, a dear buddy. Joe happened to be a member of the board at the struggling college. It was a God-ordained meeting, I always say. Dots were connected, minds percolated, and John was asked to come in and meet the board.

Neither John nor the board chair had any intentions of meeting each other before the Bravos rendezvous.

Meeting the Board for an Interview

John spent more than a few sleepless nights fervently writing his plan for a successful turnaround.

God had not only given him the plan, but many scriptures of His calling to this project. It was a marriage made in heaven.

John is a no-holds-barred kind of guy. He will tell you exactly what he thinks is needed for any plan to succeed.

We went together to the meeting. All members and the president were accounted for. Some folks he knew from ministry-business dealings, some were new to him.

It started with introductions and small talk. I could see John had ants in his pants.

"John, how do you see this college turning around?" The chairman of the board asked.

John beamed. He was on. Everything he was waiting for had come to a crescendo. He presented a no-nonsense red-to-black plan. A well-thought-out, concise direction for the future of the college. He could barely contain his emotions.

Lastly, he said, "For this to work, I would need full control of the college from the presidency down the chain."

I thought, *Here it is.* John had pooped in the pooch. It was as if John had said, "If you want me to do this, I will need the control to make it happen."

John had learned long ago that having others in command inhibited the progress needed when turning things around. He had seen too many emotional dramas when the ships went down. It was a hard line for him but a much needed one for success.

The board asked him what educational background he had for this position.

John's reply was, "Well, both my parents were schoolteachers." Yes, this was the only knowledge John had about education. Yet John, in his defense, was a well-thought-of leader in his church and community. God had been going ahead of him and He had called him.

Watching God Move

Do you know that every board member and the President himself agreed to John's terms?

When it's God's business, He calls and He equips. It is as simple as that.

All mountains are made flat. A highway is made through all the obstacles no matter what the incline.

Isaiah 40:4 (NIV) says, "*Every valley shall be raised up, every mountain and hill made low; the rough ground shall become level, the rugged places a plain.*"

Our responsibility is to take the step.

John asked me to come into the college and warm up the place.

I'm the shoe that makes you feel so comfortable you never want to take it off.

I'm the one who brings people together. Why? So we can look out for one another. In leadership, this is a vital asset to have. If your coworker knows you have their back, so much can be accomplished.

The college looked like a prison with neon-white walls and stone-cold furnishings. We spruced it up and warmed it up with a Panera-style theme. I found a beautiful world map to cover the wall with at the entrance. Everyone helped. It was a community project. We all had skin in the game. John and I had tons of fun turning that college around.

Don't get me wrong. It wasn't all daisies and daffodils. There were many ditch-digging tests too. We always prevailed when we persevered, reminding ourselves it was God's project and He would make it happen.

God is completely trustworthy. His plans will never be thwarted.

That college went from red to black. The staff and kids rejoiced as we got on the same ditch-digging page together. With God before us, who could be against us? It was all His business.

We were just His containers.

Chapter One

CLAY IN THE ALMIGHTY'S HANDS

Daniel, God's Container

"Cindy, you are not praying specific enough prayers," John challenged me on our morning walk. I could tell he was frustrated with my weak faith.

Our mornings consist of walking Willie, our dapple wiener dog, whom we affectionately call a rock star because every person who meets him kisses him on the snout or clicks a picture of him. (Not to get sidetracked, but when he was little, my vet said he should be chipped because he was so beautiful someone might steal him. Seriously, she said that to us.)

What a spectacular morning, I thought. The sunrise peeked behind our palm tree-lined road simulating the Florida posters I used to think were fake. That orange glow is as real as you pinching your skin.

The salty air felt mildly humid on my face that morning. I could smell a touch of the ocean even miles away.

John clarified what he'd initially told me during our walk. "Cindy, have you asked God to increase your social media for His kingdom by 35,000 views?"

I laughed in my heart, thinking, *There's no way. He's looney.*

John began praying on our scenic walk, "Lord, give my wonderful wife" (that's what he calls me) "35,000 views; it's for the encouragement for your people, God, please."

We finished our walk and went on with our busy day. Two days later, I received a call.

"Hi Cindy, this is Janet Brand. I just finished your book, *Tragedy Turned Upside Down*. I want to host you on Global 7.TV" (Google it).

What? Who?

"Cindy, it's inspirational TV," Janet clarified, "I'd like you to host a weekly program to encourage our viewers. Your book is full of life-giving help."

She continued, "Cindy, our world needs this kind of hope. We have 500,000 viewers!"

I sat down, cried, and laughed. God had answered John's morning prayers, despite my laughing heart.

Little Pushes

As I write this, I can't help but think of how Sarah laughed when God told her she would have a child at the ripe old age of ninety. That was me. Thankfully, God still answers prayers despite unbelief.

God still answered my husband's prayers. Within way too short a time for me. We were asked by the media station to go across the world to film the program *Treasures in the Storm*.

John said, "Cindy, we must go. God is definitely calling you to this."

I had many logical reasons as to why we didn't need to go there, *what if it is not safe? It's halfway across the world. I'm not a world traveler. I have so much responsibility here. Who will watch my Willie, our dapple wiener dog?* My practical, emotional self was digging a deep hole, convincing me how unnecessary this was.

I'm so thankful for how God uses John when I am fearful. When God calls me to something my first emotion is fear. Why? I think it's because I see my humanity; my unqualified nature rises up and my inabilities rear their ugly heads. Is this true for you too? The call is always bigger than we feel qualified to handle. Does God allow that so we will rely on Him and not our own laurels?

I was looking so far down the road I couldn't see the next step. My mind wound over and over on that little red recording light. Will I freeze? Nightly I dreamt about it.

I'm so happy John heard God's voice. I would never have gone across the globe if he hadn't pushed me. He knows me well.

So I prayed, "Lord, I know you have answered John's prayer in a big way, but really, Lord? This? I was just saying to you, God, how maybe I'll retire and not speak. I'm getting older, after all. Remember that conversation, Lord?"

I felt Him say in my heart, "Cindy, there's no retirement in my kingdom, only prosperous next steps."

I went from feeling ready to step down to fast tracked. It was all too much for me. John started with little pushes to get me moving, like the ones I used to do with our son, Adam, when he was young. I'd tell him to clean his room of 200 beanie babies and he'd melt down in tears right in front of me.

He'd say "Mom, I can't." It was just too overwhelming. Or when he would come home on the first day of school in the fifth grade and tell me, "Mom, there's 750 pages in my science book!" Another meltdown would come. That was me, 100 percent. John's end goal for me was much higher than I thought I could accomplish.

God Works Us through Our Fears

My first fear was flying across the world in the middle of Covid.

"I don't think so, honey," I said.

My husband countered, "Don't you always say there's no safer place to be than in the center of God's will, Cindy?"

Yes, I did often say that so I had nothing I could say because I believed that with all my heart. It was time to put my words into practice. So John booked the flights and I had less than a month to prepare my messages and pack for filming on television.

What do you even wear on TV? I thought. What I would wear was the lowest priority. The message was the most important thing. What was I going to say? What could I, little old Cindy, even bring to the table to encourage an audience?

My mind was consumed from the minute I opened my eyes in the morning to when I finally fell asleep at night. Over and over, a reel of fear played in my mind and my heart pounded so hard that I thought it would leap out of my chest. I actually thought I was having heart problems. This must have been what a true panic attack feels like. It was horrible. Nothing I tried stopped it. Finally, I threw my hands in the air and just went with it.

God Pushes Us to Do More than We Think We're Capable Of

The station asked me to get a prayer team together for the project. It would prove to be my lifeline. I cannot begin to tell you how God used each one of those team members in my life.

John and I met with the owner of the station via Skype. I was told to get as many messages together as possible.

"I'm only going to be there for a week. So maybe with the time change, all I could do would be ten episodes, and that's super risky."

But we were flying all the way across the pond.

"I should lay it all on the field. God will give me what's needed. This is His project. He will have to supply everything."

While at breakfast the next day, my friend Barb said, "Cindy, I hear you're preparing twenty-five messages."

What? "Twenty-five? No way. Not on God's green earth could I do that."

John told Barb's husband, Tom, that I was going to do twenty-five episodes.

That man of mine was completely crazy. Seriously crazy. Yet there was an undeniable nagging in my heart.

"God, are you calling me to do twenty-five episodes?"

I felt like I needed to push myself because, after all, I was going across the globe to film this.

I started working. If God wanted twenty-five episodes, He'd give them to me. Many friends and acquaintances prayed for me as I worked, and messages just flooded my mind one after the other, non-stop.

I ended up with twenty-eight episodes! A record was set. It was the most episodes made in the shortest time frame. Now even you, my audience, can say, "Only God."

I brought only one suitcase, a carry-on piece, with clothes for twenty-eight TV episodes. That, ladies and gentlemen, was a miracle.

We Westerners have lots of stuff, don't we? My motto was to keep it simple. God brought another woman, Barb, to help me pack for the show. She was fantastic. She gave me the confidence I needed. Her taste was similar to mine, which was helpful. We spent many hours in my bedroom closet trying many different combinations of clothes and jewelry. In the end, I didn't have to buy a single thing. She was so wise and talented at taking pictures of each outfit so I could remember what went together. It reminded me of Garanimals for kids. Remember those? They had animal tags on children's tops and pants so that kids would be able to match their clothing well.

I'm always amazed at God's involvement in the littlest of details; everything is in His fatherly hands. Barbara was my godsend. At the suggestion of another world traveler friend, I rolled my clothes, closed my case, and called it a day. I never went back to relive what I put in there. I think the biggest mistake we make is rethinking what's already been decided. In the end, it was exactly what I needed.

Only God

My heart still pounded hard for weeks. It wasn't normal for me to be so freaked out. I had done better the night before I had my double mastectomy.

John asked me how I was feeling

I said, "I feel like I'm going in for heart surgery."

I meant a real heart transplant. The constant, hard pounding in my chest never went away. In the past, I would often cry out to God and He would comfort me, but not this time. I memorized scripture. I prayed and prayed. Nothing! Not a movement toward peace. *Why, God? Why? Why not bring me peace? This is your plan. I'm being obedient, so why?*

There was nothing but a continuous, underlining panic each hour of my day as I worked to prepare the messages.

I received much advice from so many well-wishers. Prepare more. I could never be too prepared. "It will give you confidence, Cindy," said one friend.

It sounded like sound advice. I believed in having my act together. I just didn't know how much to do or what exactly to do. Many of my messages the Holy Spirit would give me on the fly. If He didn't show up, the messages wouldn't happen. It's a personal thing; it's how He made me.

In the thirty-eight years of messages He's given me, He always showed up 100 percent of the time. I'm not saying I didn't shake when I spoke. I'm saying He always showed up. The messages were not dependent on me. They were His messages He delivered, no me in it.

Fearfully, I did what I knew in my preparation to do. I put all my papers away and said, "God, you will have to do it."

That was when I finally began to thoroughly enjoy my journey.

Only God! I didn't want to miss out on His adventure for me across the globe by worrying.

We were upgraded to business class on our flight because it was as cheap as a coach ticket. Really. Only God. Unbeknownst to us, one of the blessings we received from business class was getting through all Covid checkpoints quickly. Sometimes I just have to bow my head in such wonder of God's care.

In *The Knowledge of the Holy* by AW Tozer, pg. 92 he says, "We may plead for mercy for a lifetime in unbelief and at the end of our days be still no more than sadly hopeful that we shall somewhere, sometime, receive it. This is to starve to death just outside the banquet hall to which we have been warmly invited."[1]

John and I had been invited to the banquet hall on this trip.

"Or we may, if we will, lay hold on the mercy of God by faith, enter the hall, and sit down with the bold and avid souls who will not allow diffidence and unbelief to keep them from the feast of fat things prepared for them."[2]

I want all the fat things God wants for me. How about you, dear friend?

So if my heart pounds like I'm going in for a heart transplant, so be it. Jesus is far more worth it than my feelings.

From Scotty Smith's prayer (Smith 2021),

"Heavenly Father, as odd as it sounds on this August Saturday, we are grateful for your capital G Godness. That is your absolute sovereignty and all-encompassing reign. You are the entire alphabet of providence from alpha to omega. You don't have a history of getting better at being God; you are eternally perfect. The past holds no regrets or oops for you. The future is pregnant with every good thing you planned for us in Jesus."

God Wants to Delight Us

We arrived midday just to settle in and prepare for the morning filming. What a sweet family we got to stay with. I admit that at first I was hesitant.

I am a wanting my own space kind of girl. The thought of staying with people was weird for me, especially when I had to focus on what in the world I was going to say when a little red button would turn on, and they'd say, "Action!"

This family was special, though.

They were not intrusive. We were so happy to be with them. One morning, Shayne got up. He was the husband and father of the household. (Did I tell you they have a precious six-year-old boy too?) Shayne would get up super early, head to the local bakery to get his favorite apple fritter warm out of the oven, and then he'd bring it to us in our room. Breakfast in bed. We lived like kings and queens.

That's living in the banquet hall.

By the way, it was the best apple fritter in the whole wide world. I'm dreaming about it as I write to you.

In the midst of grueling schedules for filming, we had some really fun experiences, like having dinner at a winery in the mountains, drinking coffee at trendy downtown cafes, and eating lots of very delicious homemade bread. We also had gourmet cooked meals and a delicious homemade mushroom soup, which was a favorite of mine.

What I learned: This is how lavishly the Lord wants to delight us. I could have missed all this delight if I had listened to my controlling fears, but God would not have any of that. He took me by the scruff of the neck and had a talking-to with me. "Cindy, if you will not stand firm in your faith, you will not stand at all."

Tippy Toes at the Edge of the Pool

So for you and I, we have only one option. If we put into practice what God tells us in Luke 6:46-49, then nothing, not one single thing, can shake us.

My greatest fear of all was the camera's red record button. I had been in similar situations before and I had become completely paralyzed.

I remembered these memories like they had happened yesterday. Once a news anchor in front of the White House asked me a question, and I knew what I wanted to say, but nothing came out of my mouth. Nothing.

So that was my baseline, gripping fear. I feared that it would happen again. Yet there I was going across the world to film this. Would I freeze before the camera? My friends all reminded me God wouldn't let that happen. Yet I just couldn't shake the fear. I could not believe it.

Then the moment came that I had waited for. I was in the chair and hooked up to a mic. In a few seconds, it was going to be D-Day. I was going to see my greatest fear actualized!

The camera guy told me he would clap and then I would need to start speaking.

I had heard a message from a preacher a couple of weeks earlier that grabbed hold of me. His sermon was on anticipation and expectation of God. He talked about his fearless three-year-old son who always jumped into pools because he thought he could swim. Yikes, right? This boy would put his tippy toes at the edge of the pool and then fling himself like Superman into the water where his dad was standing in the pool.

I reminded myself of this and figuratively put my tippy toes on the edge of the pool to fling all in for God. It was an invigorating feeling.

Clap, lights, camera, action!

Boom. I was speaking and all my words were flowing. It was a miracle just like my friends had said. In fact, I was so comfortable it was as if I was talking to my friends like we were having coffee together.

This went on for days until I finished all my taping.

The team said never in their twenty-five years of filming had someone done episodes in such a short amount of time with no teleprompter.

With God, all things can happen and are possible. Do we ever want any work of our own in God's enterprises? Heavens no. So we better to fling ourselves out and lay everything on the line. Let's let Him work through us for His purposes and plans even when we have no idea what they are.

Let's let the sovereign Creator of the universe decide the course of action.

Taking the Quarterback View

I am preaching to myself as I share all this. It is easier said than done.

My only regret was that I was occasionally a little short with the camera team. I'm grieved about that. They were wonderful people and who was I? A nobody. I remember feeling tense when the camera team stopped all production to have a meeting.

My fears got in the way and I became afraid my rolling ball would stop when I wasn't done with all the episodes. Funny thing was, I knew when I was about to get short with them. Although God was revealing it to me, I wouldn't let my fear go. I was bent on controlling the scenario. It pains me to say it now. *Why, Lord, can't I submit and trust You in the scary times? Oh, how I need You to intervene.*

When I take the Monday morning quarterback view, wow. Wow. Wow. I could have belly laughed at adversity and skipped to my Lou through the schedule. It was, as I always knew in my head, God's project and His work. I was just His container.

Life is so much funnier, lighter, freer, easier, and more peaceful when we leave God in the driver's seat of the car.

As you continue to read of God's supreme and sovereign goodness toward the patriarchs of God, and in my own life, I hope you will also see this applies to your life too. We have much to learn on the road to God's freedom. We want to feast at His banquet, not scrap for dog crumbs under His table. We want to play at the seashore, not play in the mud puddle.

God's Upside-Down Plan

Mark 1:9-12 (NIV) sets the scene. After Jesus was baptized by John the Baptist, the Lord God said to Jesus, *"With you I am well pleased."* Immediately following this beautiful, loving connection between Father God and His Son, God immediately sent Jesus into the wilderness for forty long days to be tempted by Satan! The scripture states that Jesus was with wild animals and the angels attended to Him.

What? *No. Wilderness, Satan tempting Jesus, and wild animals?* God's plan for His beloved Son looked absolutely upside down. *Lord, this is a horrible thing to do to your Son,* I thought.

Yet it was a brilliant plan because He was God. As Isaiah 29:16 (NIV) says, God turns things upside down, like sending Jesus to a horrific cross death to save our souls.

God's Plan for King Nebuchadnezzar, Daniel, and Daniel's Friends

In chapter one of the book of Daniel, the Lord delivered. Stop and take in the fact that the Lord delivers. He who loves you more than the sand on the seashore delivers you.

The king of Judah was handed over to king Nebuchadnezzar (or Neb, for short). The scene is set. The Babylonian king gathered the best Israelites and trained them to be his elite force of servants.

He looked especially at Daniel's group (Daniel, Shadrach, Meshach, and Abednego) because God had caused the king to show favor to Daniel.

The Lord worked behind the scenes with his perfect plan to give these elite men special knowledge and learning so they could understand visions and dreams of all kinds. God's purposeful hand was always unfolding and He was orchestrating the events of favor.

Dear reader, this is also true of our events. You and I may not understand God's reasons for our difficulties. For example, we may not understand why a friend would be disloyal to us or why sickness would attack us. But we can know God is involved and cares more deeply than we do about our suffering. He has a plan for our lives that is more precious than silver or gold (James 1).

Daniel spoke with King Neb who had experienced some disturbing dreams. The king wanted answers. Daniel told him, "I cannot interpret them, *'but there is a God in heaven who reveals mysteries,'* and He has shown me, Daniel, what the dream is" (Daniel 2:28 [NIV]).

The dream was about what would take place in the future. It involved Babylon's fall and the kingdoms that would come after.

Because Daniel was able to interpret the dream when no one else could, King Neb proclaimed that his God was the God of all gods. He also put Daniel in a high position and lavished him with many gifts. God went before Daniel and gave him favor with the king by orchestrating his circumstances for His ultimate end. However, God did not deliver Daniel from slavery. His plan was to use Daniel while he was in slavery.

Sometimes it's necessary to God for us to be in difficulty.

Where has God placed you and I today that may not be where we had hoped? Could God be using us in that difficult place like He used Daniel?

I'm taking comfort in the God of Daniel Who is the same yesterday, today, and tomorrow. The word we use is immutable, meaning never changing, already perfect, for lack of any human words for our Divine God. God's always unfolding flawless plans behind the scenes. He has people in places that He moves forward in every case, moment by moment.

Takeaways from Daniel's Story

What can we learn about Daniel's experience so far?

We can learn to place God in the center of our mess, our chaos. This is His rightful spot. This is how to keep Him supreme and how to keep us in tow.

Oh, what a satisfactory place for us to be in! What a sweet aroma it must be to our heavenly Father's nostrils when we trust His hand over all our situations.

I was just speaking with John about a situation, a text I received that was hurtful. Isn't it strange that those who are closest to us hurt us?

John and I reminded each other that God was in the center and had a good purpose. So we decided to bow our heads and walk together into that purpose. It was not easy, but because of God, we trusted His process.

Daniel 5:23 (NIV) says *"But you did not honor the God who holds in His hand your life and all your ways."*

Oh, how displeasing it must be to our Father when we live in unbelief. That's why we should preach the truth to our aching hearts and bow our sad heads to Him. Only He can make things right. He commands us to this—He who holds our lives and our ways in His fatherly hands.

Could this be why our unbelief in God is so sinful?

Daniel's Friends

In the next scene, King Neb has a change of heart toward the elite men. Instead of favoring them, he pours his wrath out on them!

What, God? Why put these servants of your Elite Team in harm's way? Why, from such kindness, favor, and support you granted in King Neb's eyes to this? Why allow the furnace to be turned up and these men be thrown into the blaze? Afterall, they would not do what Neb said and worship his golden statue.

Even the soldiers who threw Shadrach, Meshach, and Abednego into the furnace burned to death, yet not a hair on these three men's heads were touched. Not even the smell of fire on their clothes was noticed from the blazing furnace. The King, who watched all of this, called to them, *"Servants of the most high God, come out!"* (Daniel 3:26 [NIV]).

The king saw that while the men were in the furnace, a fourth person walked around with them who looked like a son of gods. The king realized this was a miracle. A miracle of God Most High. So he said, *"Praise be to the God of Shadrach, Meshach and Abednego, who has sent his angel and rescued his servants! They trusted in him and defied the king's command and were willing to give up their lives rather than serve or worship any god except their own God"* (Daniel 3:28 [NIV]).

King Nebuchadnezzar must have felt envious of these men's complete devotion to their God. He must have thought, *If only I could have such devotion given to me.*

After this happened, the king promoted Meshach, Shadrach and Abednego. He also honored God Almighty.

God's plan is always to exalt Himself to His proper position. He desires ultimate glory and supreme authority. He wants His people to know they can trust Him. He wants them to see where their confidence can come from. He deserves their honor.

What we learn about God and these men is that the Christian life is not always one of ease and protection. It's one of living life to the fullest on the edge of God's cliff, because this is the safest place on earth.

"The thief comes only to steal and kill and destroy; I have come that they may have life, and have it to the full" (John 10:10 [NIV]).

Lord, help me to believe just a little of what these men believed about You and walk as they walked the tightrope of faith triumphantly.

The Monster of Unbelief

Charles Spurgeon, in his Morning and Evening Aug 27th, said: "Strive with all diligence to keep out that monster unbelief. It so dishonors Christ, that he will withdraw his visible presence if we insult him by indulging in it.

It is true it is a weed that we can never entirely extract from the soil, but we must aim at its root with zeal and perseverance ... Its injurious nature is so venomous that he who exerciseth it and he upon whom it is exercised are both hurt thereby ...

This sin [our unbelief] is needless, foolish and unwarranted. Jesus has never given us the slightest ground for suspicion ...

It is shameful to doubt Omnipotence and distrust all-sufficiency. The cattle on a thousand hills will suffice for our most hungry feeding, and the granaries of heaven are not likely to be emptied by our eating ...

Who can drain a fountain?"[3]

So let us together strive to smash to smithereens that monster of unbelief.

God's Plans for Nebuchadnezzar

After these pre-planned experiences of God took place in Nebuchadnezzar's life, things went super well for him. He started to praise the one true God. He was on point. Listen to what he said after his encounter with God: *"King Nebuchadnezzar, To the nations and peoples of every language, who live in all the earth: May you prosper greatly! It is my pleasure to tell you about the miraculous signs and wonders that the Most High God has performed for me"* (Daniel 4:1-2 [NIV]).

The scripture reminds us that one of God's purposes in our suffering and in our unhappy circumstances is to bring us to a more complete knowledge of His love, His sovereignty, and His completeness. Also, He accomplishes His good purposes within our calamities so we can fully trust Him, our supreme God.

I love how King Nebuchadnezzar mentioned that God did all these wonders and signs for him alone. God became his personal God. I wonder what wondrous gifts God has brought to us, even though at first we see them as filthy, ripped-up carboard boxes.

If we look back at this story, Nebuchadnezzar tried everything to get rid of these three men. Although they were gifts of God, King Neb saw them as a thorn bush. Yet these three men were very miraculous gifts God was presenting to him.

This begs us to ask ourselves, could our hardest aches become our greatest joys?

James 1:2-4 (NIV) states, *"Consider it pure joy, my brothers and sisters, whenever you face trials of many kinds, because you know that the testing of your faith produces perseverance. Let perseverance finish its work so that you may be mature and complete, not lacking anything."*

Lacking nothing means we are complete. Completely satisfied with all things under God's care for us. A truly delightful, happy, free, content place of joy.

There was much more work to be done in King Nebuchadnezzar's life.

The first part of Psalm 119:67 (NIV) says: *"Before I was afflicted, I went astray."*

Another Dream

After all this goodness and prosperity, God brought the king another gift.

This one was a little more painful than the last. The king had another dream.

Daniel 4:5 says that this dream terrified him.

You know, the kind of nightmare you just can't get off your mind, the one you feel traumatized by, the nerve-wracking one that ruins your day?

King Nebuchadnezzar called all his enchanters and astrologers to interpret his dream, but no one could until Daniel came along.

Interestingly, we see that the king left godly counsel from the one true God and sought out worldly advice and counsel from enchanters and astrologers.

Take note for yourselves. Do not leave godly advice for foolish or worldly wisdom.

The dream said that King Nebuchadnezzar would be driven away from people and he would live with animals. He would eat grass until he could acknowledge that the most high God was sovereign over all the kingdoms of the earth and that He was able to give kingdoms to anyone He wished.

Wait. Didn't the king just proclaim that to the nations? What happened?

God's goal for King Nebuchadnezzar was that he would give glory to God and acknowledge that His dominion was eternal. This could only be accomplished through him living with wild animals and eating grass.

Daniel 4:33b-35 (NIV) states, *"He was driven away from people and ate grass like the ox. His body was drenched with the dew of heaven until his hair grew like the feathers of an eagle and his nails like the claws of a bird. At the end of that time, I, Nebuchadnezzar, raised my eyes toward heaven and my sanity was restored ... [He declared] All the peoples of the earth are regarded as nothing. [God] does as he pleases with the powers of heaven and the peoples of the earth. No one can hold back his hand or say to him: 'What have you done?'"*

The passage goes on to say, *"Now I, Nebuchadnezzar, praise and exalt and glorify the King of heaven because everything he does is right and all his ways are just"* (Daniel 4:37 [NIV]).

What a beautiful aroma this was to the Lord's nostrils.

This was the upside-down gift of God. It was the blessing of all blessings to know God this way and believe His ways were just and right.

God Shows Us the Truth in the Darkness

The Lord has quite a way of showing us the truth when we're off the reservation, doesn't He? What might He be doing in our circumstances today? Could He be wanting to get our undivided attention back on what's true and right and lovely and praiseworthy and most excellent? Might He want to transport our broken hearts and wayward souls back to His tender, fatherly care?

Our dark seasons can bring a Nebuchadnezzar-like deliverance, a joy we always wanted but didn't know we needed. I used to think my thought-out, every-scenario until Tuesday was the best logical path, the only right path.

I'd tell myself, *walk in it, Cindy.*

Since then, I have learned and now I remind myself that I am not God. Although I do not know all the exact answers to life's problems, in hindsight, like the king, I can say, *Everything God does is right and all His ways are just.* This is the accomplishment of God in our darkness.

I'm now dedicated to preaching daily to myself when the hard times hit. It's the way out of my suffering.

For instance, I had lunch with a dear friend whose adult daughter overdosed and died this year, which was so heart-wrenching. My friend is doing well because with everything in her, she believes this truth and has put it in the mind of her soul. She is preaching the truth to herself. What truth? God is in this tragedy. He loves her daughter. He does what's best. Only He understands what's good for this precious daughter and my hurting friend. Her peace and confidence exude out of her. I am praising God because of her settledness. I see contentment in her eyes. Thank you, Jesus!

Daniel's God

The king's next generation forgot a very important message the Lord sent through King Nebuchadnezzar.

Belshazzar, Nebuchadnezzar's son (more likely his grandson), inherited the kingdom. He would have had vivid memories of how God dealt with his father, yet he refused to humble himself and fell into the same sin as his father. You would think he'd have a little fear of God after hearing of Nebuchadnezzar's suffering at the hand of God over his unbelief.

How easy it is to become complacent and blend in with worldliness. We convince ourselves God doesn't see our sin. *It's really just an unhealthy habit. Everyone is doing it.* We preach death to ourselves so we can continue in sinful, ungodly ways.

Scripture declares that King Belshazzar followed in his father's footsteps of praising the gods of silver and gold, bronze and iron, which could not see, hear, or understand. Daniel told King Belshazzar, *"But you did not honor the God who holds in his hand your life and all your ways"* (Daniel 5:23 [NIV]).

God Holds You in His Hands

Take a moment to acknowledge the one Who holds in HIS hands your life and all your ways.

How can you acknowledge God in the center of your circumstances today?

For me, it is Covid. Both my husband and I just finished a horrific bout of that deadly virus.

John was in the hospital for ten days. He is a man in stellar health, a runner, and a committed exerciser. He eats well. He's the last person on earth to end up in a hospital. Yet he spent ten days there. After Covid, he was a shell of a man. He looked like my mom who wasted away from cancer. His eyes bulged because his face was so thin. You've probably seen that before in cancer patients who are so emaciated.

Every day was a fight for breath as he sat in his lazy boy chair with his O2 Machine pumping oxygen into his damaged lungs.

How did we get here, Lord?

I know too well we were not alone in our nightmare. I had heard and seen many who struggled with Covid like John did. So many families lost lives. Yet this was not an accident to God. He knew what was best. He had not forgotten or forsaken us. No. No. I had seen this before in my life and I had learned to bow my head in full trust of the One Who held in His hands my life and all my ways.

Let us remember the words of Daniel 5:23. God has proven His love for you and I too.

In extremely tragic days when everything looks so wrong and when my pain feels unbearable, I remind myself God will never forsake me. He will never let me go. He promised.

As John was fighting for his life in the hospital and I was alone at home sick with Covid, the Lord brought to my memory a Psalm I taught myself, Psalm 121. When I was scared to death and my heart pounded out of my chest, and when I was frightened in the middle of the night, all alone, I would slip out of bed onto my knees and look to the heavens. I would cry out to the Lord and point my finger up to Him. I liked to do that when making a point. I recited back to my heavenly Father all His promises from memory.

Psalm 121 (NIV) says, "*I lift my eyes to the mountains—where does my help come from? My help comes from the Lord, the Maker of heaven and earth.*" (I pointed my finger to where my help comes from while on my knees!)

"*He will not let your foot slip—he who watches over you will not slumber; indeed he who watches over Israel* [*that's you and me*] *will neither slumber nor sleep.*"

(I kept pointing my finger, reminding myself of God and of His promises.)

The Psalm goes on, *"the Lord is your shade at my right hand; the sun will not harm you by day, nor the moon by night."* (Day and night, HE'S watching.)

"The Lord will keep you from all harm—he will watch over your life, the Lord will watch over your coming and your going both now and forevermore."

Wow. wow. wow. How I needed the reminder at that moment. I got up off my knees, slipped into bed, and quickly fell into a sweet sleep.

That's God's power in our fragile emotions when we lift our eyes to Him.

John and I are fine today. We together say Covid was God's good gift to us. We learned so much about HIS love in how He brought our way doctors who knew us, to nurses who knew us, to a hospital bed we didn't deserve to have during the height of Covid, to friends and neighbors who brought us food in both the hospital and on our doorstep.

Our wonderful son flew in to care for me and my Covid-infected home. We had people praying from across the country to across the world. We didn't deserve any of it. Yet it was in the Sovereign's love to do this. We have asked the Lord to help us remember His gifts in Covid, the treasure chest we call our toolbox for trials, more so than all the scary, painful moments.

We are much closer to the Lord now because through Covid we saw our sin of self-sufficiency and our prideful control in own our lives as well as in others' lives. God was creating a purer heart in us so we could see Him better.

"Blessed are the pure in heart, for they will see God" (Matthew 5:8 [NIV]).

John says he's squishy now. He means that he's less tense about life's concerns. I see more joy in him today than I did before he had

Covid. This, my friends, is just the tip of the iceberg of goodness from a hard thing.

As James says, we should consider it pure joy when we suffer trials ...

Those are awfully strong words. We are to have pure joy in our suffering. I'm learning to grab hold of those words.

1 Corinthians 13:12 (NIV) states, *"For now we see only a reflection, as in a mirror; then we shall see face to face. Now I know in part; then shall I know fully, even as I am fully known."*

Back to Belshazzar

Daniel didn't want any of it, but King Belshazzar clothed him in fine purple and put a gold chain around his neck. He made him the third largest ruler in the kingdom (Daniel 5:29).

We see firsthand God's powerful plans for the hearts of men who are affected by His causes.

What a humble, surrendered servant Daniel was. He had no interest in exaltation, comfort, or freedom. He had just simple, strict loyalty to his great High Priest.

He was what I call a container for the most high God.

What can we learn from Daniel 5? We must stay devoted and loyal to our God. He will rescue us from all foes. As we will see later in the chapter, Daniel was spared from death when many Babylonians (including Belshazzar) were killed.

The very best place, the safest place, is to be in the center of where God wants you. So stay true, stay put, do not waver, and do not waffle.

The same sentiment seems to be echoed in Joshua.

Joshua 1:9 (NIV) says, *"Haven't I commanded you? Be strong and courageous. Do not be afraid; do not be discouraged, for the Lord your God will be with you wherever you go."*

This verse was such a comfort to me when my dear friend was diagnosed with colon cancer. The Lord gave her this verse. She put it solidly in her mind and in her heart and quoted it often during her illness. I would also recite it with her. Jan had three beautiful boys, five, ten and fourteen years old. Her illness progressed rapidly. I came to visit her in the hospital one day and through many tears we wrote letters to her wonderful boys.

After she passed, I remember going to the park with her boys and reading the letters to them. At that moment, I was so grateful we had spent the grueling time getting them written. That verse kept Jan in God's peace as she battled for her life. There is something about God when He gives us a word. It washes over our shaking souls.

Daniel and the Lions

Daniel was distinguished among his peers, the administrators. He had exceptional qualities. The king's plan was to put him in charge of the entire kingdom. This infuriated the rest of Daniel's cohorts, so they tried to trip him up, and stumble him.

The problem was that Daniel was full-on when it came to integrity and character. He could not be coerced. So the cohorts devised a plan.

They went to King Darius (the king at the time) and asked that the people only pray to him for the next thirty days. Daniel would never compromise his worship of God Almighty to pray to a king.

Daniel's devotion makes me stop in my tracks. Am I that devoted to King Jesus?

Daniel got wind of this and went before the Lord God in prayer. "Help me, Lord." It was a simple, profound, and powerful request. The punishment for disobedience against King Darius was to be thrown into the lion's den.

Wow! Quite a harsh retribution for not bowing to a king and praying to him. Death by lions mauling you. I wonder if I would have compromised.

I would have to say, *yes, yes, yes!* Of course, I would. The stakes would be way too high. Death by mauling? Seriously?

Cindy, you just have thirty days of this crazy King Darius and then you can go back to worshiping your Yahweh, the only true God. This is the lack of integrity God is trying to show me.

Lord, today, where do I justify, because my life's on the line, that it's ok to not worship You and to have other gods before me?

Selling Out

My life's not on the line, and yet so many times, I sell out my soul for a bowl of stew as Esau did. If you haven't read that story, check it out in Genesis 25.

Just yesterday, I planned how to sell out God. I schemed how to not admit to my tennis team that I lead a Bible study, which was why I was late for the year-end luncheon. Instead, I would tell my teammates the study was an encouragement group. That was a complete sell-out moment. *Forgive me, God.*

Worse than that, I dialogued with my Bible study before the luncheon about how it was okay to compromise, and it was actually godlier to do so because the tennis team could be offended with the words "Bible study."

Of course, I didn't use the word "compromise" because I knew better than that. Not much better, though. Thankfully, I later shared this grievous sin with my Bible study group. Since then, many of the women have been very clear when sharing at golf, in the hospital, or at a book club that they are going to Bible study. I'm grateful they could learn from my grievous sin.

How often do we keep Jesus in our box? Or how much do we struggle admitting to our neighbors that we're on our way to church? Or how about why we are not gambling at the local neighborhood casino night party?

Lord, help! I love You, God. Keep me from ever being embarrassed by You. Help me to acknowledge You inside and out in all that is happening in my day. Give me a pure heart, Lord, please.

Daniel's Faith

When King Darius heard that Daniel would not comply with bowing in prayer to him, this greatly grieved him because he loved Daniel and did not want him to get hurt. But the king had to execute the punishment set in his own law. So he threw Daniel into the lion's den and locked the door.

The king couldn't even eat his dinner that night. He stayed awake and tossed and turned over his decision. The next morning he ran to the lion's den and yelled, *"Daniel, did your God protect you?"* (Daniel 6:21 [NIV]). Check out Daniel's response.

"Daniel answered, 'May the king live forever! My God sent his angel, and he shut the mouths of the lions. They have not hurt me, because I was found innocent in his sight. Nor have I ever done any wrong before you, Your Majesty.' The king was overjoyed and gave orders to lift Daniel out of the den. And when Daniel was lifted from the den, no wound was found on him, because he had trusted in his God" (Daniel 6:21-23 [NIV]).

It's amazing what happens when we trust and have faith that is even as small as the smallest seed.

Mathew 17:20 (NIV) states, *"Truly I tell you, if you have faith as small as a mustard seed, you can say to this mountain, 'Move from here to there,' and it will move. Nothing will be impossible for you."*

The reason Daniel was spared (Daniel 6:23) was because he trusted in his God. Oh, that you and I would trust God as Daniel did in our own troubles.

Those manipulators who falsely accused Daniel were brought in and thrown into the lion's den along with their wives and their children. Those are hard words of truth to pen. The scripture says, *"And before they reached the floor of the den the lions overpowered them"* (Daniel 6:24 [NIV]).

The king then wrote to all the living nations at the time (Daniel 6:26-27 [NIV]):

"Issue a decree in every part of my kingdom. People must FEAR and REVERENCE the God of Daniel. For he is the living God and he endures forever, his kingdom will not be destroyed, his dominion will never end.

He rescues and saves; he performs signs and wonders in heaven and on the earth. He has rescued Daniel from the power of the lions."

God's plan is always in accordance with His character and is always the very best for all involved. We see through the glass dimly, but God sees with crystal clarity, much like the sun shines on a clear blue sky at noon.

God's goal: Every person would know the truth of His supremacy. Not a dust particle runs across our table that hasn't been filtered through His fatherly hands. Each speck is strategically placed.

So today, let us approach His throne with confidence for our petitions.

Questions

1. Daniel was unwavering in his devotion. Where have you been steadfast in your commitment to God?

2. Where may you have fallen short in your devotion?

3. Where can the church tighten up its devotion to Jesus?

4. How have you been faithful or unfaithful in your sphere of influence?

5. How have you felt others wanting you to compromise your walk with Jesus? What can you do to shore up your commitment to Jesus?

6. Have you ever been asked to deny Jesus? Write down how God spared you.

7. What does it mean to fear and reverence God?

8. What do fear and reverence look like in your present circumstances?

9. What steps can you take to increase your devotion to God?

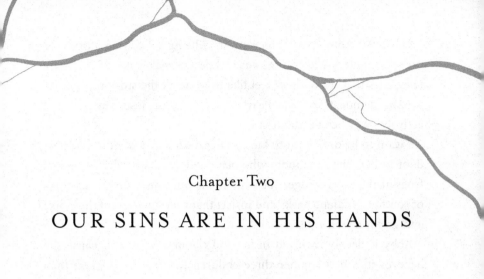

Chapter Two

OUR SINS ARE IN HIS HANDS

Abby's Life

My dearest friend called to say her beautiful and godly daughter, Abby, was caught drunk out of her mind.

What? What? What? She doesn't even drink. Not Abby. No, never. She is a righteous woman of God. Gifted in so many areas for the kingdom of God.

Abby is a forty-five-year-old woman who speaks of Jesus all day long. I call her a true evangelist at heart because she reaches out to anyone she meets. She is a friend to the most distant stranger, especially to the down and out. She loves those who struggle deeply from her heart.

Abby is passionate for orphan wives.

A wife and mom herself, she engages with those who are discarded. I have watched her speak into hurting women's hearts. You name it; she's about all things Jesus.

We call Abby "poster mom" because of how lavishly she loves her brood of three.

You'd want to visit Abby at dinnertime because of the aroma coming from her kitchen. It permeates the entire cul-de-sac, you know, like when your neighbor is grilling delicious steaks. I've had dinner at her house and I'm number one in her fan club.

However, Abby's real superpower is being a bedtime storyteller for overnighters who gather near while she makes up wild, fantasy fairy tales that make them feel like they are in the story too.

Abby demonstrates the Pearl of Great Price, Jesus, in how she actively loves her neighbors.

I want to be one of those kids on her dead end. I want to live next door to her. She's the mom who plays volleyball after dark or hunts frogs at the pond's edge. She's the mom who camps in the foothills of southern Indiana parks and insists that everyone get on their bike and go for a trail ride.

Abby is deeply involved in her kid's homeschooling because she believes it is best for her three children that she loves more than life itself.

Maybe you're a mom like her, or maybe you desire to be that kind of mom.

Her husband calls her blessed and desires what God wants for her in their marriage. A family favorite game is playing hide-and-seek in the dark while running the trails in the thick forest of southern Indiana. At night, s'mores are on the family menu. But only after one of Abby's fabulous campfire meals.

If you walked into Abby's beautifully decorated, warm, shabby chic country home, you'd find God's word dangling from her walls and fixtures. She is a true warrior of God. Her love for our Savior is pure and real. Abby is convinced that Jesus saves lives along with souls.

You would never know this, but early in Abby's life, she was a hard-core drug addict.

Abby should not be alive today. But by God's mercy, He delivered her by His divine intervention as only He could, and she was made new. She had a 100 percent transformation.

Completely Transformed

Salvation makes someone completely transform, the old passes away and a new person comes alive.

Some stories of salvation are harder to tell than others, but Abby wasn't reluctant to share hers. If you heard her story and saw a before and after picture, you'd know God did a miracle. She'd often speak to women about her drug addiction and how God delivered her from bondage. How her life was now hidden in Him, and she was protected, free, and alive. She wanted God to deliver others as she had been.

God freed her *"from the jaws of distress to a beautiful spacious place"* (Job 36:16).

She was forever grateful for His compassion and His lavish love which she said she least deserved.

A passage from AW Tozer says what Abby knew about Jesus beautifully; "The goodness of God is that which disposes Him to be kind, cordial, benevolent, and full of goodwill toward men. He is tender-hearted and of quick sympathy, and His unfailing attitude toward all moral beings is open, frank, and friendly. By His nature, He is inclined to bestow blessedness and He takes holy pleasure in the happiness of His people."[4]

When God does something so unbelievable and so unexpected, you just can't stop being thankful. That's how Abby felt.

So how could this drunkenness be happening in this godly woman? How could she plunge into this trap? I began hearing stories of her being wasted. It sounded like a horror movie; not real life, especially not Abby's life.

I prayed, *How, Lord, does this wonderful, Jesus-centered woman of God fall so far so fast?*

You may know of stories like Abby's. The rumors come in all around you. I decided I would be speculating if I gave any opinion on how this could have happened. It would be pure conjecture.

God's View Through Paul's Story

What I do want to highlight—when thinking about hard stories like this—is Paul's life in the scriptures. Let's gain a picture of God's view on the matter.

I grieved with Abby's mom, a best friend of mine. I gave solution after solution for the problem. All my best efforts, fervent prayers, and best guesses. In the end, God will have to fix the broken.

Some say, "You don't want to just lay down and leave it all up to God. God helps those who help themselves, right?"

What I have to say is let's look at Paul's circumstances and see what we can gain from God in Paul's life. Then, let's apply it to Abby and her family and then to our lives and families.

Paul's sins were in God's hands.

God preplanned Paul's life before he was ever born. This is true for you and me also.

What's hardest to comprehend in Paul's story is how God used even the most sinful areas of Paul's life for HIS purposes.

Let's dig in. In Acts 9, Saul (Paul) breathed out murderous threats against the Lord's disciples and against God's anointed and chosen servants. Paul's passion in life was to fervently persecute and kill Christians!

In Galatians 1:13 (NIV) Paul states, *"For you have heard of my previous way of life in Judaism, how intensely I persecuted the church of God and tried to destroy it. I was advancing in Judaism beyond many of my own age ... I was extremely zealous."*

He was zealous against God's people!

That's what I call an intense passion for evil. Could this be worse than the terrorists of today?

Now not to confuse you, but Paul had two names, Saul and Paul. I'd change my name too if I had murdered God's anointed and then later showed up to evangelize to them.

Yes, that's what happened.

Acts 13:9 (NIV): *"Then Saul, who was also called Paul ..."*

It's known that dual names were common in those days. *What?* What were those mothers thinking?

Saul was looking for men and women who belonged to Jesus so he could take them as prisoners to Jerusalem. As he neared Damascus on his murderous journey, suddenly, the Lord met him on the road.

He asked Saul, *"Why, Saul, are you doing this horrible thing to me and my people?"* Saul, overwhelmed and scared to death asked, *"Who are you, Lord?"* (Acts 9:4-5 [NIV]).

The scene was set. God was about to change him from having a stony heart to having a heart of flesh. Saul's evil, wicked, nasty, sin-filled soul was about to be miraculously transformed on that dusty road to Damascus.

Saul never had an inclination to want to know Jesus before that day. He had no interest in a changed heart and had no idea that he even needed a new heart. He never concluded that he was a sinner in need of a Savior. His sole motivation in life was to persecute Christians. He was vehemently against anything that had to do with Jesus. His desire was to kill and imprison anyone who named the name of Jesus. The last thing on earth he wanted was to belong to the "way", as it was called.

But God. *"No purpose of [God's] can be thwarted"* (Job 42:2 [NIV]). Even the vilest murderer is putty in God's hands.

God saves people while they are still sinners who want nothing to do with Him. Just like Saul, He saves them while they don't even know they need a Savior.

Romans 5:8 (NIV) states, *"But God demonstrates his own love for us in this: While we were still sinners, Christ died for us."*

While we were still dead in our sin, when we wanted nothing to do with Him, that was when Jesus died for us.

Unfolding the Plan

It's God's plan to save a people like you and me for Himself in His own way. He does all the heavy lifting.

Look how Jesus unfolded His plan.

He met Saul/Paul on the road to Damascus and shined a bright light in his face, which blinded him. He instructed him to go to the city and follow His instructions.

We find out in the scriptures that the Lord planned and saved

Paul's soul for the purpose of using him to bring the Gentiles into the kingdom (Acts 9:1-22).

I wonder what God's plan is for me? I wonder what His plan is for you?

I'm sure Saul/Paul wondered too. Saul's experience with Jesus on that road left him speechless. Can you even imagine such an interaction with our living God?

I have a friend whose husband was struck by lightning and lived to talk about it. I wonder what he thought about God's plan for his life.

(If you have ever had a similar experience, I want to know about it. I will definitely put it in my next book).

As Saul/Paul was likely wondering what God would do next, another man entered the story. In Acts 9:15 (NIV), the Lord told Ananias (one of his disciples), *"This man [Saul] is my chosen instrument to proclaim my name to the Gentiles."*

Ananias freaked out. It's as if he said, "WHAT, Lord? I have heard many reports about this man and all the harm he has done to Your holy people. He has come here with authority from the chief priests to arrest all who call on Your name. He's Your chosen instrument, Lord?"

It was clear from Ananias's words that Saul did not want Jesus as his Savior (as we call it when someone makes a decision for Christ). There was no decision. It was not this man's choice or his intention to receive anything. Quite the opposite. He was dead in his sin. But what we see is it was our almighty, all-powerful, orchestrating God Who decided Saul/Paul's fate.

In Acts 22 (NIV) we are given a smidgen of insight into what God had planned for Saul/Paul: *"Go to Damascus; there, you will be told all that you have been assigned to do."* A few verses later, we find out Paul's mission from Ananias (God's instrument to speak to Paul and give him his sight back.)

Ananias told Paul: *"The God of our ancestors has chosen you to know his will ... You will be his witness to all people of what you have seen and heard"* (Acts 22:15-16 [NIV]).

This man, really God? Not who I would have chosen, I thought.

Ananias felt the same way.

But as we will see, God's way was brilliant, as God's ways always are.

As we evaluate the Road to Damascus story, a question arises.

When did God decide Saul's fate?

Get ready to be wowed!

Paul tells us in Galatians 1:13-16 (NIV): *"For you have heard of my previous way of life in Judaism, how intensely I persecuted the church of God and tried to destroy it. I was advancing in Judaism beyond many of my own age among my people and was extremely zealous for the traditions of my fathers. But when God, who set me apart from my mother's womb and called me by his grace, was pleased to reveal his Son in me so that I might preach him among the Gentiles ..."*

Don't miss what he says in verse 15: "when God, who set me apart from my mother's womb ..."

So the answer is God set Saul/Paul apart to be His chosen instrument while he was still in his mother's womb.

While that's all nice and good because God is God and does whatever He pleases—what about the fact that this chosen instrument killed Christians? How can that be? How can a chosen instrument from birth commit such a grievous sin against God?

The very idea is mind-blowing.

As I let this fact sink into my mind and heart, a comfort wells up inside of me. Despite the evil that is happening in my friends' lives, family's lives, and in my country, God is there. My God loves you and me so much that He allowed the excruciating suffering of His Son. How can this be?

I now have hope for all of it. God was moving in the midst of Paul's decisions.

God sets you and me apart. He calls us. He pre-plans our very lives. He even uses our sin for His good purposes.

So, I Can Keep Sinning Then?

If you think you want to just go on sinning because God is using it for good ...

No! No! May it never be. Paul tells us this in Romans 6:1-2 (NIV), *"What shall we say, then? Shall we go on sinning so that grace may increase? By no means! We are those who have died to sin; how can we live in it any longer?"*

Some may say this teaching gives us an excuse to sin. First, this is God's living word spoken to us.

Look at this metaphor. Pretend we believers in Jesus are apple trees. The thing about apple trees is that they bear apples. They must bear apples because they are apple trees. Same with us Christians; we cannot keep sinning because the Holy Spirit Who lives in us convicts us of sin and gives us the joy of repentance. We apple trees will always bear life-giving apples.

And as "apple trees" we have a mission.

Saul/Paul reminds us that he was called and saved to preach Christ to the Gentiles (Galatians 1:16). We find out at the end of Galatians 1 that all this grievous sin occurred so that the Gentiles could believe in Christ and be saved.

What? God used Paul's killing of Christians and his hatred of Jesus to show the Gentiles a miracle transformation in Paul's life. He went from an enemy to a completely devoted follower of Christ preaching about Jesus, the Savior of the world.

In Galatians 1:22-24 (NIV) Paul says, *"I was personally unknown to the churches of Judea that are in Christ. They only heard the report: 'The man who formerly persecuted us is now preaching the faith he once tried to destroy.' And they praised God because of me."*

Only God could perform a miracle in someone's life as magnificent as this. The same is true today for everyone to whom Christ gives a new heart.

You in God's Hands

God is just as involved in our lives as He was in Paul's life.

Psalm 139:16 (NIV) tells us that *"all the days ordained for* [*us*] *were written in your book before one of them came to be."*

Daniel 5:23b says that God holds you in His hands: your life and all your ways.

What a peace it is to know that my grievous sin, or the sin of my dear friend's daughter, Abby, is not outside of God's sight.

I wonder when God delivers Abby from the jaws of her drug addiction if she will speak to drug addicts about how Jesus is their Savior. Was this decided while she was in her mother's womb as it was with Saul? I don't know about Abby's tomorrow, but I'm learning about the God of her tomorrow.

As we think about the God of tomorrows, let's introduce another illustration.

Think of it this way. The Milky Way galaxy is 104,000 light-years across, containing one hundred billion stars.[5] To count them one by one, it would take us over 3,000 years. According to the latest probe by the Hubble space telescope, there are hundreds of billions of galaxies in God's universe. God brings out their host by number every night. He calls them by name so that none of them are missing. This is the God Who has promised Himself to you and me.[6] Do you think this God deserves your confidence? Do you think this God, who manages the universe right down to the faintest star, will lose track of you? (Isaiah 40:26).

From pg. 248 in *Preaching the Word* by Raymond C. Ortlund Jr., he says, "Oh, that we could stop looking at God through our own eyes! He won't look big enough for your overwhelming problems through our vision of him."[7]

God is inviting us to turn our perceptions around and see everything from His point of view.

When we are overcome with our problems, then "behold our God," the God of the one hundred billion galaxies Who brings each star out and calls them by name. He's the One we need in times of trouble.

I'm so full of hope today because of what I'm learning about our big God.

God's Glory Shines

Paul considered himself the worst of all sinners. This makes Jesus' salvation of him all the more glorious in our sight—mission accomplished.

John Piper, in his YouTube video, "Why Does Evil Exist," talks about God in His wisdom creating the wicked for a day of trouble so that His glory will shine more deeply.[8] God is completely without sin.

In Galatians 1:21-24 (NIV) Paul says, *"Then I went to Syria and Cilicia. I was personally unknown to the churches of Judea that are in Christ. They only heard the report: 'The man who formerly persecuted us is now preaching the faith he once tried to destroy.' And they praised God because of me."*

Maybe Abby will be known as a drug addict who turned to Jesus, and all who hear about it will be amazed and because of her testimony, they will put their trust in Jesus.

The fact that Paul persecuted Christians solidified in the Gentiles' minds that this must be the one true Savior of the world. Who else could bring such a transformation into someone's life? That sounds like shining glory to me.

Some Takeaways from Paul's Life

God chose Paul to be His instrument to preach to the Gentiles that salvation is from Jesus. This calling was given while Paul was still in his mother's womb. Early in his life, Paul killed Christians, yet he was the chosen one by God from birth. How can this be? Because God decided it to be so.

He saved Paul/Saul while he wanted nothing to do with HIM.

Romans 5:8 (NIV) says, *"While we were still sinners, Christ died for us."*

The sin he committed was in the plan of God. Why? The scripture says it was so that the Gentiles would hear a testimony from an evil man, a Christian killer, who turned to Jesus and became a preacher of the way. Talk about a transformation. This was to bring salvation to God's chosen Gentiles. Galatians 1:23-24 (NIV) says, *"The man who formerly persecuted us is now preaching the faith he once tried to destroy. And they praised God because of me."*

God during the Fall

Pause with me to see through scripture some of the ways of God. May God grow more glorious and more magnificent in our minds as we study these passages together.

Let us look at the well-known story of the fall of Adam and Eve in the garden.

A resource to check out is Monergism.com's article "Did God's Decree Bring About the Fall?" when looking into God being in the first big mess in Scripture, Genesis 3.

"[God] could have just as easily decided to prevent the fall ... but He didn't ... God did not make man sin coercively [but] he certainly ordained such events to occur. Consider that if God did not decree the fall, then evil is something completely outside His sovereign control ... If evil came into the universe by surprise for God, ... then there are some things He does not know or things He is powerless over, and therefore God would, by definition, lack omniscience and omnipotence. [Knowing everything and unlimited power.] ... then how do we know whether He will be able to defeat evil in the future if evil is outside God's control even though the Scripture plainly says that God ordains all events that come to pass ..."[9]

Ephesians 1:11 (NIV) says, *"In him we were also chosen, having been predestined according to the plan of him who works out everything in conformity with the purpose of his will."*

God Is in the Details

God does rule and reign over every detail.

As Paul says in Romans 9:11-13 (NIV), *"Yet before [Rebekah's] twins were ever born or had done anything good or bad in order that God's purpose in election might stand: not by works but by him who calls—she was told, 'The older will serve the younger.' Just as it is written, "Jacob I loved, but Esau I hated."*

"Esau I hated"? WHAT, God?! But You love everyone You create.

"What then shall we say? Is God unjust? Not at all! For he says to Moses, 'I will have mercy on whom I have mercy, and I will have compassion on whom I have compassion.' It does not therefore depend on human desire or effort, but on God's mercy" (Romans 9:14-16 [NIV]).

God decides. He surpasses all. He's more powerful, paramount, commanding, and mighty than we make Him out to be in our modified understanding of Him. His compassion, mercy, and love are beyond lavish, beyond our reasoning out from our less than heavenly perspectives—or as my friend says, our limited brains.

He has a specific purpose for His creation. This is our chance to see His supremeness as God. Yet He's completely without sin.

Verses 17 and 18 emphasize this when the Lord says to Pharaoh, *"'I raised you up for this very purpose, that I might display my power in you and that my name might be proclaimed in all the earth.' Therefore, God has mercy on whom he wants to have mercy, and he hardens whom he wants to harden."*

There is so much I don't have eyes for. I cannot see God's plan. I cannot see the future. How can I know what's best?

It is God's plan, purpose, and wisdom that prevails. Mine is incomplete and lacks infinite love. Someday when I get to heaven, as you will, we'll see the full story, and I promise you we will all completely agree with God's plan.

In this passage, we are asked (verse 20), *"But who are you, a human being, to talk back to God? Shall what is formed say to the one who formed it, 'Why did you make me like this?'"*

Limitless

Today, I quoted this verse to my dear friend, Abby's mom, because things are not good. Abby went back on drugs after having been off for two months and after she had been holding a promising job.

We bowed our heads to God, Who holds Abby in His hands and asked Him to forgive us for our lack of hope and trust.

After I did this, I was looking at YouTube for videos about Nick Vujicic, a man born with no arms or legs. He's always saying that God made him that way. Today, he's living life to the fullest. He's golfing, he's diving, and he's even married with children. He often says his life is better than other people's lives because he's living life fully. He's bursting with life every moment.

God made him that way. Nick could have laid in a bed all his life and the public would be okay with that because he's disabled. But Nick chooses to live as abundantly as God intended him to. Nick breaks all barriers. He says the word "handicap" means there's a limitation. He claims that he doesn't live with limitations. One of his books is called, rightly so, *Limitless*.

God is sovereign over Nick's life, over Abby's life, and over your life. We are HIS workmanship. Nick's testimony beautifully demonstrates God-size glory.

We may sometimes be tempted to question our Creator and His plan for our lives.

How can we say we think things should be different? I have a feeling if we knew what God knows now, we would do things the very same way He does it. We are not the Creator. What can we make from nothing? Only God is the Creator.

Paul makes another very valid point by simply saying in Romans 9:21 (NIV), *"Does not the potter have the right to make out of the same lump of clay some pottery for special purposes and some for common use?"*

Yes, God has every right to decide the fate of every person He has created. Let us bow our heads to our supreme leader, God, Who loves us with such a sacrificial love that He allowed His very only

Son to die for us so that we could live forever with Him. Let us trust that He has it all brilliantly worked out for us as well as for Himself.

Maybe Nick would say, "If I had been born with arms and legs, I would not have had this abundant life." Maybe he would say, "I wouldn't have grabbed hold so tightly to what I had, and I would have looked at what I didn't have." I don't know.

Maybe he'd say, "I wouldn't know my Savior as well as I do if I had legs like you."

Through Paul's Eyes

Paul finishes his story with Philippians 1:22-24 (NIV), *"If I am to go on living in the body, this will mean fruitful labor for me. Yet what shall I choose? I do not know! I am torn between the two: I desire to depart and be with Christ, which is better by far; but it is more necessary for you that I remain in the body."*

Then in Philippians 4:12-13, he goes on to say, *"I know what it is to be in need, and I know what it is to have plenty. I have learned the secret of being content in any and every situation, whether well fed or hungry, whether living in plenty or in want. I can do all this through him who gives me strength."*

He was content with whatever God was doing to him and for him. He said he learned this over time and affliction. He had to work at it; God didn't just initially pour contentment over him.

How do you and I learn contentment? As defined by Webster's Dictionary, to learn means "To gain knowledge or skill by studying, practicing, being taught, or experiencing something."[10]

People learn throughout their lives.

Just like Paul learned through all his hardships, you and I can learn through all our circumstances.

Paul ended by saying, *"I can do all things through Christ who strengthens me."* We'd be well off to keep that in our minds' toolbox to pull out when we feel the waters of life rising against us.

As I think about Paul's life, I think about the situation with Abby. What I am learning is to put God in the center of this chaotic mess.

I have a feeling that very soon she will be living in her God-given calling from birth.

Thank you, Lord, for Paul's life that I can lean into. I can't wait to see how God plays it out.

Deuteronomy 32:4 (NIV) says, *"He is the rock, his works are perfect and all his ways are just. A faithful God who does no wrong, upright and just is he."*

Questions

1. What have you learned from Paul's life?

2. What have you learned about God's ways that you did not know before?

3. How can you look at your life's circumstances as Paul did?

4. What encouragement did you receive from God through this story?

5. How can you take all that you have gained from this reading into your life this week?

6. What scripture or passage can you memorize and meditate on over the next few days?

Chapter Three

JONAH AND FRANKLIN, REBELS WITH A CAUSE

I picked up Franklin Graham's book *Rebel with a Cause* because I wanted to know his before and after story.[11] I love the Grahams. I obviously don't know them personally. But you know when people ask that question, "If you could meet one famous person, who would it be?" Mine is Billy Graham.

Although I will have to meet him in Heaven, I just can't get enough of him and his family's life stories. It's so fascinating how God used this very special family. This man went from a bad boy to a super saint. I thought the Grahams' stories would be a good parallel for the book of Jonah, and it turns out I was right.

Franklin's book starts out with a profound statement in the introduction. He says, "What is important about my story is important about every person's story: God has a plan for each of his children, and he will bring that plan to successful completion. That makes every person very special—whether or not you happened to be born into a famous family." Amen.

Franklin was a high-spirited, taller than an average adolescent. Adventure lurked around him as he searched for his next escapade. The more thrilling, the more excited he became. You know the type of person. He was one of those kids who always pushed the parental envelope, knew no boundaries, and often got into trouble. He was a risk-taker who hung off treetops and rode dirt bikes over high jumps (without a helmet).

Franklin loved living without boundaries. He loved the woods. It was his sweet spot, the place where he felt whole and alive. He lived for camping or any trail-blazing adventure he could drum up.

Rules were only guides to Franklin, something to challenge rather than something to follow. He felt energized when pushing boundaries. He gravitated toward classmates who were rule pushers like himself. You can only imagine the heartache this caused to those close to him and to those who cared about him so much.

Despite this, Franklin had a sincere respect for his elders, especially for his Daddy and his Momma. He was taught "yes, ma'am," and "yes, sir," as proper etiquette when talking with those older than himself. Yet even with this respect, his rebel streak continued.

In his teens, Franklin began smoking and drinking. Any new shiny experience was another way he bucked the system. His Christian schools gave him much grace because, after all, he was Billy Graham's son. Franklin viewed his famous family as a perk as well as a curse. He was kicked out of a few schools during his formative years because of his unwillingness to follow the rules.

Everything changed when Franklin went to work.

Franklin loved traveling so much that he was put in charge of his father's worldwide travel for Billy Graham ministry. He learned much about the political atmosphere as well as the social atmosphere during his work at the Graham ministry. He met many dignitaries because of this international work.

Franklin became deeply burdened for those hurting in war-torn countries, including those in Egypt, India, and even Syria. God was preparing him for his life's calling.

Franklin was in Israel when he experienced the Lord calling him, which led to him committing his life to follow Jesus. His father had told him weeks earlier, "Son you're going to have to make a choice either to accept Christ or reject him. You can't continue to play the middle ground. Either you're going to choose to follow God and obey him or reject him."[12]

Chapter 9 of Franklin's book starts out by saying, "God finally sent a hitman after me. His name was David Hill. He came to get me in 1972."

Sounds like God. He gives us just what we need to get us on the right track.

"David read scripture to me ... it's an agonizing situation, and who on earth can set me free from the clutches of my own sinful nature? I thank God there is a way out through Jesus Christ our Lord."[13]

Franklin said he felt frustrated as he listened to David talk.

"I realized for the first time that sin had control over my life. I wanted what David Hill had. I wanted what my parents had."[14]

That night all alone in his hotel room, Franklin read through the gospel of John. When he read John 3:3-7 he realized he had to be born again. The next few days after reading this passage, his daddy's words haunted him. He knew he had a big, empty hole inside of him and he was tired of running. In that far-off land, Franklin got down on his knees next to his bed and asked God if He would put him back together.

"I told him I want to live for him,"[15] Franklin stated. It was finished. All his running had ended. God saved him. The Rebel had found the cause.

Rebels Finding Causes

Franklin Graham had a calling on his life. God was orchestrating his circumstances to prepare him for the task he was called to accomplish. The same thing is true for you and me. We have a calling and God will make sure we fulfill it.

Ephesians 2:10 (NIV) states, *"For we are God's handiwork, created in Christ Jesus to do good works, which God prepared in advance for us to do."*

Philippians 2:13 (NIV) says, *"For it is God who works in you to will and to act in order to fulfill his good purpose."*

Franklin, like the prophet Jonah, initially wanted nothing to do with this work. He ran hard, fast, and far.

His poor mother and father. *But God.*

I say that because He is so faithful to grab the scruff of our poor, lost necks and set us on a the right road. The blessed road where our true treasures lie. Thanks be to God for that.

Today Franklin leads many large ministries, Samaritan's Purse being one of them. Just like his father, he has met most presidents and has dined with and met dignitaries in open and closed countries.

Thank you, Lord, for Franklin and for holding in your hands all his days. You are the one that makes us yield. Thank you for giving us hard things like the hard paths that show and teach us the right road, the blessed narrow path. The truest life.

I highly recommend Franklin's book. It has strengthened my confidence in my personal journey. I've learned about parenting, rebelliousness, and God's sovereign ways in others' lives. It has many lessons, and it is very enjoyable to read. I laughed and cried and now I'm singing "I've got the joy, joy, joy".

I've got that joy, joy, joy down in my heart ... because of God's supremacy through Franklin's story. Thank you, Franklin, for writing to us your story.

Packing Our Bags

Jonah's story looked a lot like Franklin's story.

Jonah's blueprint was designed by God, his architect.

The Lord specifically asked Jonah to go to Nineveh and preach against it *"'because its wickedness has come up before me'"* (Jonah 1:2 [NIV]).

If only Jonah would have listened to God. It was an easy, simple, straightforward task. Yet Jonah decided instead to flee as far away as he could possibly go and even paid a fare to get on a ship bound for Tarshish.

Now that's packing your bags! That is what I call taking your ball and leaving.

Yesterday my dear friend told me her four-year-old son put clothes in his backpack and proceeded to run away from home. Have you ever done that, little or old? At every age, we can feel like this life is not for us; like it's too heavy a bag on our backs. We run into the arms of another life. We run to where we think the grass is greener and life feels lighter, freer, funner, maybe easier.

Today, we do that by drowning our sorrows in a bottle of alcohol or taking prescription drugs, etc.

But there's one monumental problem with our scenario. We're not the architect. We are not the designer of our life.

Yes, we may act or we feel like it's all in our hands, probably much like Jonah did. We may feel we have all the authority to do whatever we please with ourselves. However, God makes these simple facts. He says, *"We make our plans freely, BUT God directs the steps"* (Proverbs 16:9, my paraphrase).

"All the days ordained for me were written in your book before one of them came to be" (Psalm 139:16, NIV).

"He is the rock. His works are perfect, and all his ways are just. A faithful God who does no wrong, upright and just is he" (Deuteronomy 32:4 [NIV]).

To be sure, this means God clothes lilies and feeds birds (Matthew 6:26, 28). But He also makes lightning (Psalm 135:7) and kills mighty kings (Psalm 135:8). Our God holds sway over the good, the bad, and the ugly. *"'I form light and create darkness, I bring prosperity and create disaster. I, the Lord, do all these things'"* (Isaiah 45:7 [NIV]).

So much for thinking that we got it controlled or that we can rule and reign over our stuff, our children, our spouse, our friends, or our country. We might as well unpack our bags.

Jonah, of course, didn't unpack. Jonah had one goal—to flee from God.

I don't know where he got the idea of running. What made him think he could escape?

Franklin, too, thought he could escape, but God brought him back. God fulfilled His plan for them both.

I am brimming with hope from learning this. God has myself, my family, my friends, and my country in His hands.

As I mentioned earlier, I've been singing: "He's got the whole world in his hands. He's got the whole world in his hands," I've been singing this to my very famous dapple wiener dog, Willie. He loves it, and he even howls as I sing to him.

What is this doing for me? It's lightening the heavy burdens that I've been carrying on my back. It's reminding me Who's got my problems, and it ain't me. So I can do the Snoopy dance!

The One Who knows every hair on my head (Luke 12:7) and the One Whose presence I can't flee from (Psalm 139:7) has got me covered.

So let's unpack our bags and save ourselves the heartache that comes from running.

Are We Like Jonah?

Maybe I'm more like Jonah than I care to admit.

God asks me to do something, such as forgive a person I hurt or worse, forgive someone who hurt me. What do I naturally do?

I run away as fast as an Olympic sprinter.

I tell myself that God might forget about it, not truly care about it, or eventually leave me alone. I tell myself that He's so busy with more important things, and that it's not really necessary for me to forgive. Although I know I have wronged someone, I continue to minimize the situation and maximize how unessential forgiving them is.

This sounds completely irrational when written on paper, doesn't it? I just ignore what God asks me to do. It is absurd.

As insane as this all sounds, Jonah wanted nothing to do with sparing the evil Ninevites. No matter what God told him to do, he remained set in his thinking.

God asked Jonah to preach to his sworn enemy. He even asked him to preach deliverance to them.

Has God asked you to do something hard too?

Recently, a friend asked me what she should do about a situation. Her best friend suddenly stopped talking to her, a friend she'd had for twenty years. When she went to her friend's home to ask what the matter was, her friend's only response was, "I have other friends."

My poor friend had lost her forty-something daughter and was still grieving. She was so hurt, angry, and sad. A month later, she went back to her supposed best friend and asked again, "Please tell me what I have done? I'm so hurt because of the loss of my dear and only daughter."

The stone-cold woman just folded her arms and repeated, "I have other friends."

My friend's question to me was, "What do I do with my friend?"

The answer? "Pray for her."

Stepping toward your enemies and praying for them is one of the most difficult things Jesus asks us to do.

"But I say unto you, 'Love your enemies, bless them that curse you, do good to them that hate you, and pray for them which despitefully use you, and persecute you'" (Mathew 5:44 [KJV]) ... The NIV says, *"I tell you, love your enemies and pray for those who persecute you."*

Perhaps she must have thought in her heart "I will never be nice to her. I will never forgive her. I'm so bitter towards her and I deserve to be." All I can do is be the friend that when they get to heaven were glad I was their friend. We have to let God's words fall on those struggling for He alone can make our words a healing balm.

How Jonah Felt

This must have been how Jonah felt.

In fact, when God spared the Ninevites he said, *"Isn't this what I* said, Lord, when I was still at home? That is what I tried to forestall by fleeing to Tarshish. I knew that you are a gracious and compassionate God, slow to anger and abounding in love, a God who relents from sending calamity" (Jonah 4:2 [NIV]).

It sounds like Jonah wanted nothing to do with forgiveness. It seems like he wanted a big dose of revenge on the Ninevites. Do you ever wonder what they might have done to him? We know from the scriptures they were an evil people. They would have been hard to forgive.

Do you ever feel like an enormous dose of revenge is exactly what's needed for the wrong done to you? Is the thought of God forgiving your enemy abhorrent to you? God wanted to bring mercy and love to the Ninevites. Jonah just wanted a piece of their hide.

I get it, do you? Some just don't deserve forgiveness in our eyes.

Oh wait, that would also include you and me.

Jesus came and delivered you and me from sheer destruction. He brought us while we were still dead in our sins to a spacious place with no restrictions to HIS table laden with choice food. Now that's undeserved (Romans 5:8 and Job 36:16).

Lord, when it is hard to forgive, please put forgiveness in my heart because I cannot do it unless you give it to me.

Lately, I have been consoling a friend who lives with a difficult husband. Frankly, she's miserable, lonely, and hates her life. This poor woman is consumed with gloomy, pathetic, and unhappy thoughts. I'm so sad for her because of what she is missing out on. I feel her pain, but I also know God is in the center of her hard suffering (1 Thess. 5:18 and Romans 8:28).

I have been asking God to do this very thing for her.

Like Jonah, my friend thinks her husband deserves punishment for how he's treated her, and maybe he does. This is not an abuse case. That would be a very different scenario. This is a wife who's having real trouble trusting God with her circumstances and who's struggling with asking Him to help her find any sliver of good or any grateful moment.

We all know someone like this. Perhaps we are that someone.

We've been in situations like this. We feel for people like my friend because we know how hard it can be. In Alistair Begg's article, he shares how to reach contentment.

"What Paul says in Philippians 4, as you noticed, was, "My circumstances have ebbed and flowed, I've been in coach. I've flown in coach in the back of a DC-9 right by the jolly engine with no window, and I've flown in first—"and I've learned"— whether I'm in first or I'm in the back row of the DC-9—"to be content." That's for us to learn.

This is how to be content whether where we prefer or decline. I try to remember that when I'm stuck in a middle seat on an airplane or on a bunk bed at a friend's house.

What first world problems."[16]

I know this example pales in comparison to a super hard marriage. It is not equal, for sure, but I do hope it gives a glimpse of hope to those in the middle of a trial.

Anger to Hope

How can we move from bitterness to hope?

First, we must accept what God has ordained for us. Second, we must find every tiny morsel moment by moment to be grateful for. Third, we must ask the Lord to give it to us, and He will.

There's a passage in *Jesus Calling* that helps remind us to do all three of these things:

"WHEN YOU ARE PLAGUED by a persistent problem—one that goes on and on—view it as a rich opportunity. An ongoing problem is like a tutor who is always by your side. The learning possibilities are limited only by your willingness to be teachable. In faith, thank Me for your problem. Ask Me to open your eyes and your heart to all that I am accomplishing through this difficulty. Once you have become grateful for a problem, it loses its power to drag you down. On the contrary, your thankful attitude will lift you up into heavenly places with Me. From this perspective, your difficulty can be seen as a slight, temporary distress that is producing for you a transcendent Glory never to cease!"[17]

Let's look in Isaiah 30:20-21 (NIV) for further encouragement.

"Although the Lord gives you the bread of adversity and the water of affliction, your teachers will be hidden no more; with your own eyes you will see them. Whether you turn to the right or to the left, your ears will hear a voice behind you, saying, 'This is the way; walk in it.'"

I love pouring truth over our circumstances.

Don't you wish Jonah had ears to hear so that he could have seen God's purposes for good? Imagine all the misery he could have been spared.

Saving Us from the Storm

Jonah, of course, was content to wallow in self-pity and to run away from God. But God was not going to allow him to do that.

God controls every single cell of our universe. As only He can, He sent a violent storm with powerful winds to Jonah while he was on his boat to Tarshish.

Could God have been saying, "I'm going to love Jonah right where he would benefit from it the most?"

Jonah 1:4 indicates the storm was so violent that the sailors started praying to their foreign gods.

"... such a violent storm arose that the ship threatened to break up. The sailors were petrified, crying out to each other "call on your own god. Maybe he'll save us from this perilous storm." Jonah had slept at the bottom of the boat. You know why? Because Jonah knew the storm was brought by God for him. He'd had resigned himself to his fate (Jonah 1:12 [NIV]).

Those poor victims. The ship's crew and the captain eventually realized that the cause of the storm was Jonah and his God.

Jonah explained to the crew that his God was the one true God, the Lord God, "the God of heaven, who made this sea and the dry land" (Jonah 1:9 [NIV]). This terrified the men ...

They realized that Jonah's God, the Lord God, was infinitely greater and mightier than their gods.

What to do? They reasoned, "let's try and make it to land." Unable to do so, they decided the only option was to throw Jonah overboard to drown. That or everyone else would perish.

But what would this powerful, almighty God have to say about murdering Jonah? The men had quite a dilemma. As a last resort, the crew cried out to the Lord in Jonah 1:14-15 (NIV), *"please, Lord, do not let us die for taking this man's life ... for you, Lord, have done as you pleased ... and they took Jonah and threw him overboard and the raging sea grew calm."*

Even the sailors who had no knowledge of Jonah's sovereign God feared Him, offered sacrifices to the Lord, and made vows to Him. The ship's crew believed in Jonah's God as the only God. All this was the result of Jonah being thrown overboard.

If the sailors had succeeded in murdering him, killing Jonah would've been an evil, sinful, murderous act. Yet God sovereignly used the situation to bring this group of sailors to know Him, the one true God.

I wonder what God could be doing in our upside-down situations. What could He be doing even through evil acts, sinful acts, or murderous acts?

I have given much thought to this extreme act. Our supreme God had preplanned Jonah's story.

Jonah was to preach to Nineveh. Jonah, furiously angry at the thought, revolted and literally sailed away.

BUT GOD, Who will have His way and His plan 100 percent of the time, had nothing that could thwart Him. Not any person, situation, false god, or devil.

I'm so thrilled to know this, especially when my circumstances are screaming Save me from this wretched mess. My God is personally watching and acting in all life's drama.

He was involved when my son died and when I was diagnosed with Hodgkin's disease and later breast cancer. He was involved when my mom died and when my dad died. He worked all things out for His supreme good and our supreme good. Thank you, Jesus. *Lord, if You would have told me in advance all that was going to happen, I'd tell You to send someone else. No way. But having been through it all, hard and devastating at times, You, Heavenly Father, have always been next to me, holding me with Your strong and righteous right hand.*

Oh, that we could know HIS constant willingness to act in our best interest 100 percent of the time.

God's Plans Are Never Thwarted

In Peter's sermon to his fellow Israelites in Acts 2:23 (NIV) "*[Jesus of Nazareth] was handed over to you by God's deliberate plan and foreknowledge; and you, with the help of wicked men, put him to death by nailing him to the cross.*"

It was clearly God's deliberate plan and foreknowledge to put Jesus to death.

Proverbs 6:16-17 (NIV) tells us that God hates "hands that shed innocent blood." And yet He sent His Son to suffer a bloody fate. Is this a mystery? Absolutely. But it is not nonsense. We can look at evil and with no contradiction say, "This is wrong, and God has willed that it takes place."

"*There is no wisdom, no insight, no plan that can succeed against the LORD*" (Proverbs 21:30 [NIV]).

"*The Lord foils the plans of the nations; He thwarts the purposes of the [wicked] peoples. But the plans of the Lord stand firm forever, the purposes of his heart through all generations*" (Psalm 33:10-12 [NIV]).

We can write that in stone. It's a fact. A promise of God.

As Isaiah 30:20-21 reminds us, sometimes the Lord gives us the bread of adversity and the water of affliction ... yet we will have counselors, teachers, and tutors at our side.

God let Jonah get into serious trouble on that boat. He even had his fellow sailors throw him into a raging sea to accomplish His purposeful, perfect, holy, righteous plans. We learn that all the sailors abandoned their gods to worship and fear the one true God, Yahweh. Interestingly, this all happened because of Jonah's rebellion.

Just a quick recap: God took Jonah's disobedience and had him murderously thrown into the sea. This was all so the ship's crew would acknowledge Him as the one true God and worship Him.

God uses all necessary means to accomplish His heavenly purposes—sin, rebellion, even wickedness.

Proverbs 16:4 (ESV) states, *"The LORD has made everything for its purpose, even the wicked for the day of trouble."*

God Provides

Jonah was thrown into a raging sea. The crew just threw him overboard to save their necks.

Get ready to be wowed. The Lord PROVIDED a huge fish to swallow Jonah (Jonah 1:17). You may have heard this story before but think about how crazy that is.

A big fish ate Jonah. Can we read this any other way? Or is it a coincidence that a big fish swallowed Jonah? No, the scripture says that God provided the fish. Provision is a thing needed because we lack something. The Latin origin *providere* means foresee, attend to. God attended to Jonah's ultimate needs by providing a huge fish to swallow him.

The Lord kept him in that fish for three days! While in the fish, Jonah spoke with God. *"In my distress, I called to the Lord, and he answered me"* (Jonah 2:2 [NIV]).

Interestingly, while in the raging storm on the boat, Jonah was sleeping. Not even a violent storm was enough affliction on him to turn him. God knew it would be inside of the belly of a fish where Jonah would find his greatest need. It would only happen through God's upside-down provision. Jonah said, *"from deep in the realm of the dead, I called for help ... YOU [God] hurled me into the depths into the very heart of the seas"* ... he had currents swirling, and waves and breakers sweeping over him. He said he was banished from God's sight. *"Though engulfing waters threatened me, the deep surrounded me;*

seaweed was wrapped around my head," though he sank down to the roots of mountains, that is where he proclaimed, "*Salvation comes from the Lord*" (Jonah 2:2-5 [NIV]).

God was the provider of Jonah's horrific conditions. Such conditions God skillfully planned with pin-pointed precision to masterfully do what HE desired in Jonah's life. Mission accomplished. Jonah came running at warp speed to where he knew, beyond a shadow of a doubt, his only help could come from—GOD.

Scripture tells us time and time again that we often turn to God when we're in strange circumstances. Psalm 121:1-2 (NIV) says, "*I lift up my eyes to the mountains—where does my help come from? My help comes from the LORD, the Maker of heaven and earth.*"

Jonah said it was God Who sent the storm, God Who threw him overboard, and God Who had him swallowed by the fish.

Jonah understood that God was supreme over all his circumstances. Yes, even the less than desirable ones.

Lessons Learned in the Fish

What Jonah learned in the fish.

1. God will make sure I get to Him. He has His ways.

2. Sometimes it takes great suffering to bring us around: "*When my life was ebbing away I remembered you Lord*" (Jonah 2:7 [NIV]).

3. It's pointless to pursue idols. "*Those who cling to worthless idols turn away from God's LOVE for them*" (Jonah 2:8 [NIV]).

Jonah left obedience to God for a worthless thing: his own way. He did not want mercy for the Ninevite people. He thought they should be destroyed.

Jonah sounds a lot like other people in the Bible.

Another Bible character who wanted his own way was Esau. He sold his rights for a bowl of stew because he was hungry (Genesis 25:29-34).

It doesn't take much to run from God or His will for you.

Jonah left God's will because of unforgiveness and a lack of compassion for the Ninevites. It wasn't because of an affair, or gambling, or greed, or wanting another's job, house, kids, wife, husband, or car.

He left God for an empty cistern in his soul.

His passionate disregard for Nineveh shriveled him up, as we will see later in Jonah's story.

Satan presents God's will as something trivial, insignificant, unimportant, and a hindrance to our desires. May we be able to see the foolishness in both Jonah and Esau and refuse to trade our birthright in for something far less valuable.

A Poem

As we think about God's sovereignty over our circumstances ... and the temptation to run away when life gets hard, read this poem, and let it remind you of God's truth.

A simple poem to remind us
When we're off the reservation.

Two choices on the shelf
Please God or please self.

If I please God, I will feel:
joy, peace, contentment, fulfilled, light-hearted, serene.

If I please myself I will feel:
empty, downcast, defeated, inflated, sad, depressed.

Ask yourself, how will I feel if I do this?

Making Good

Although Jonah didn't have this poem, he did have his prayers, which reminded him of God's character. While in the fish, Jonah began to see his God again. He said, *"But I with shouts of grateful praise will sacrifice to you"* (Jonah 2:9 [NIV]).

He vowed to the Lord he would make good.

Through God's direct providence, Jonah came back to the rightful calling of his life. He was lead back to his first love through a provided fish to eat him! *Hmmm!*

He thanked God, praised Him, and sacrificed to Him, along with making a vow to do what God commanded him and to make right what had happened. Then and only then, *"The Lord commanded the fish, and it vomited Jonah onto dry land"* (Jonah 2:10 [NIV]).

Jonah's story isn't over. There's still two chapters left in the book. But let's stop at this midpoint and ask ourselves some questions.

Questions to ask ourselves:

1. Where do we see ourselves in this story? Is there a fish coming? Maybe we are already in the fish.

2. What is God wanting us to do? How can we become obedient before God brings a provision of love to us?

3. God could have picked Jonah up and cleaned him off and given him a grateful and submissive heart. Why do you think He didn't do it that way?

So many of us learn the hard way. I wonder if Billy and Ruth Graham wondered why God didn't bring a big fish into Franklin's life earlier, or why God didn't just pick him up, clean him off, and give him a heart for Jesus.

Franklin did say God brought him a hitman. We also know that all that hard stuff was growing Franklin for the ministry ahead of him.

At first, it seems like Jonah is in it 100 percent, ready to resume his calling, just like Franklin was.

Jonah was all systems go for obeying God. His heart was cleaned and he was ready for the righteous road. God asked Jonah again to *"go to the great city of Nineveh and proclaim the message I give you"* (Jonah 3:2 [NIV]).

God pre-prepared the way and hearts of the Ninevites to believe in Him. Jonah preached, and everyone believed. A fast was proclaimed in Nineveh, just as God had planned for these people He cared so much for. The king of Nineveh got wind of Jonah's message from the Lord and decreed for everyone to call urgently on God, give up their evil ways, and do away with their violence. The king said, *"Who knows? God may relent and with compassion turn from his fierce anger so that we will not perish"* (Jonah 3:9 [NIV]).

At Jonah's preaching, all the people, even the king of the country, repented and turned to God.

Amazingly, when God asks us to do a thing, He's going to have authority and control over every outcome, even when it looks upside down to us. Therefore, the outcome is His, not ours. We look through glasses dimly. God sees with precision. Isaiah 55:8-11 says that God's ways are not our ways. They are better, heavenly, and far more superior than what our finite minds can understand. This is a paraphrase of these verses.

Happily Ever After?

Jonah obeyed God and Nineveh was saved. That sounds like the best way to end the book of Jonah.

You might even end this story with a happily ever after.

We expect Jonah to be compliant, moldable, and submissive to the Lord's direction. After all, he had a Damascus Road experience while in that large fish. God redirected his life, and he was finally on the righteous road preaching to the Ninevites. He had a perfect ten out of ten in fulfilling the Lord's will.

Then comes chapter 4 and the sludge at the bottom of the pond thickens.

Immediately, we find that Jonah was angry over the people's repentance. Scripture says, *"But to Jonah this seemed very wrong and he became angry"* (Jonah 4:1 [NIV]).

What? What happened to Jonah's perfect ten compliance? His heart being submissive? His fantastic preaching to the Ninevites and all their repentance? Was it just a show? Was it half-hearted? Did he not fully submit to God's direction for him?

"Isn't this what I said, Lord, when I was still at home?" Jonah said (Jonah 4:2) (In reference to before the fish experience). *"That is what I tried to forestall by fleeing to Tarshish. I knew that you are a gracious and compassionate God, slow to anger and abounding in love, a God who relents from sending calamity"* (Jonah 4:2b [NIV]).

Jonah recognized God's lavish love, His great compassion, His long-suffering, and His graciousness. He knew that the Lord did not become easily angered.

Interestingly, Jonah mentioned that God relents from sending disaster. This is the same guy who God put in a fish for three days. I don't know about you, but I'd call that a colossal calamity.

Yet Jonah knew it was a necessary event for God's fish to swallow him up. By Jonah's very accurate representation of God—he acknowledged that He was loving, compassionate, and slow to anger. Yet there he was, angry as snot, furious and outraged that God would be so wonderful and gracious to the Ninevites.

I feel like Jonah more than I care to admit. For example, just last night, the Lord wanted me to have dinner with a nice couple. John, my wonderful husband, set it up.

I was so stinking tired of having a completely full-in-my-face day of ministering to people and helping them with their problems that I couldn't even see straight. I found myself plotting to get out of the whole evening invitation. I figured I could plead my case for a sore throat. That would definitely scare the strongest of countenances away, considering Covid and all.

No fish had swallowed me up yet. I looked around, thinking about Jonah's story as I plotted my escape. However, I did end up going to that dinner.

John told me the couple wanted to have an early dinner. I prayed, "God, please wake me up. Give me a good attitude."

I was not a happy camper. The house was in Timbuktu, forty-five minutes out into the back roads of what felt like the hills of Kentucky minus the hill part. We arrived promptly at 5:30 at a lovely, well-lived-in, farm-style home on a serene plot of land. It had ponds, knee-high corn, as well as cats, dogs, and geese running around.

I wonder how many farm animals called that place home.

The owner welcomed us in and apologized for his wife who was still getting ready. We sat outside and enjoyed the summer breeze along with each other's company. It couldn't have been a more beautiful evening. The sun was slowly setting before our eyes.

Yes, as spectacular as the evening was, I would have given my hind teeth for jammies and a Hallmark movie. However, this dinner was God's will, and it was His priority for John and me. John had put in a long, hard day of meeting with clients, so neither of us were ready to be social.

Our eyes caught each other. Where was the wife? It had been forty-five minutes, and still, no wife. We were supposed to eat, make niceties, and leave.

Finally, Sue came out to the porch and apologized for taking so long to get ready. "Fastest she's ever cleaned up," her husband said.

What? I don't know about you, but if I need to be ready lickety split, a good fifteen is plenty of time. I was already on the crazy misery train of my mind. No grace or love was in me at all.

We shared some pretty deep life stories given it was our first time meeting Bob's new wife. We had much in common, both having had breast cancer. We enjoyed their company. God had been gracious to John and me, giving us energy and motivation to be present in our conversations with them.

Time was ebbing away. It was 8:15. There was still no food, and we were still socializing. John and I exchanged glances again.

Are we having dinner or not?

The husband got up from his chair and said, "I think I'll start the grill."

What? Now? The grill? Pork chops? No?

I prayed in my head, *Lord, I knew You would have this dinner go on* and on because You care so much for this couple and have something so special for them.

Dinner was finally served at 9:00ish. It was way too late for a meal of any kind. I was a linn-er person. Lunch and dinner together, linn-er, at 4:00 in the afternoon.

John and I graciously scarfed the food down as if we'd never had a meal. Then came more socializing, more sharing, and more encouraging them in their new blended family dynamics. Honestly, I was looking for a fare to pay to flee to Tarshish. The whole time I had to remind myself, *Cindy, this is God's will for you tonight.*

Maybe we are all more like Jonah than we care to admit. Like Jonah, I learned my lesson that night.

Thanks in All Circumstances

One of my life verses from the Bible is 1 Thessalonians 5:18 (NIV), *"Give thanks in all circumstances; for this is God's will for you in Christ Jesus."*

The evening finally ended at that late dinner, and we journeyed into the pitch dark forty-five minutes back to civilization. Our mission was accomplished. I only had to keep a good attitude in the morning when I knew I'd be exhausted.

Many of you are relating to my frivolous pity party because we all have things in our lives God calls us to that, well, we would really rather not do.

Jonah was no different than the rest of us.

Is there a BIG fish coming to swallow you? What is God asking of you that you've decided is an absolute no?

Dear friend, it's only a matter of time before God WILL have His way. As the Lord says in Isaiah, *"Woe to those who go to great depths to hide their plans from the Lord, who do their work in darkness and think, 'Who sees us? Who will know?' You turn things upside down, as if the potter were thought to be like the clay! Shall what is formed say to the one who formed it, 'You did not make me'? Can the pot say to the potter, 'You know nothing'?"* (Isaiah 29:15-16 [NIV]).

It is God's plans that prevail 100 percent of the time.

Believe in God and know that no plan of His can be thwarted! The meaning of "thwart" is "to hinder, obstruct, frustrate or defeat a person's plans, etc. ..."[18]

There is no wisdom, no insight, no plan that can succeed against the LORD" (Proverbs 21:30).

Still Running

We can know God's goodness and still run.

We are called to bow our heads in a "Yes, Lord" posture. His will is the only will that matters.

What amazes me is that for all Jonah had learned about God, HE STILL RAN. His next sentence in Jonah 4:3 (NIV) was so dramatic: *"Now, Lord, take away my life, for it is better for me to die than to live."*

This must be what happens when we are bitter. A hatred appears deep in our souls to the point of us wanting to die rather than help the party who has offended us. This kind of hatred can come only from a very personal offense.

Yet God wanted something so much more for Jonah. The same is true for us.

The scripture says that an offended brother is more unyielding than a fortified city (Proverbs 18:19 [NIV]).

I imagine this applies to a spouse of twenty years who has an affair and the other spouse catches them in the act.

John and I watched an episode of a favorite show of ours, in which the husband made a career of helping struggling businesses. When his wife discovered his affair, she became so angry and vividly furious. She was scary.

It had gone on for three years. A long amount of time. I couldn't imagine her hurt. She had opened her very vulnerable heart to someone who was supposed to care for her, but when she turned her back, her husband stabbed her in her heart. Maybe that's how Jonah felt, maybe his heart turned hard like the wife on that show.

The Lord responded to Jonah, "Is it right for you to be angry?" (Jonah 4:4 [NIV]).

Well, I guess not. He's the potter and I'm the clay. He's the Creator. He has authority and is the God above all gods. I exist to bring HIM all honor, glory, reverence, and supremacy.

Charles Spurgeon explains it this way:

"Upon some points, a believer is absolutely sure. He knows, for instance, that God sits in the stern sheets of the vessel when it rocks most. He believes that an invisible hand is always on the world's tiller and that wherever providence may drift, Jehovah steers it. That re-assuring knowledge prepares him for everything. He looks over the raging waters and sees the spirit of Jesus treading the billows, and he hears a voice saying, "It is I, be not afraid." He knows too that God is always wise, and, knowing this, he is confident that there can be no accidents, no mistakes, that nothing can occur which ought not to arise."[19]

Well, I guess it's not right for Jonah to be angry. It's also not right for me to be angry when my life feels topsy turvy or when unwanted guests arrive unexpectedly to my perfectly planned life.

When I say unwanted guests, I am speaking of my breast cancer, the death of our miracle son, my father's Alzheimer's, and my mom's lung cancer. The list is long and frighteningly hard. BUT God! As we clearly see here in Jonah's life, these perfectly planned providences are more precious than silver or gold in our lives. James 1 (NIV) tells us to *consider it pure joy, my brother, when you face trials of many kinds.*

God's Object Lesson

"Jonah had gone out and sat down at a place East of the city" to watch what God would do after Nineveh's repentance (Jonah 4:5 [NIV]). In the meantime, God provided a leafy plant to grow up over Jonah to comfort him from the heat: *"Jonah was very happy about the plant."* But at dawn *"God provided a worm"* to eat the plant so that when the sun rose, *"God provided a scorching East wind."* Jonah grew faint

under the oppressive heat and became angry about his shade being pulled out from under his feet. He was weary enough to die. God said to him, *"Jonah, is it right for you to be angry about the plant?"* (Jonah 4:5-9 [NIV]).

Jonah's response was *"'It is,'"* and *"'I'm so angry I wish I were dead'"* (Jonah 4:9b [NIV]).

I wonder if Jonah had forgotten everything he had just learned. How could he forget he had just been swallowed by a fish and yet survived in its belly for three consecutive days? Did Jonah's misery take control over his faculties? His judgments about his circumstances seem crazy.

Do you ever wonder if we too have these moments of insanity when life is so messed up and we are so angry that we lose all sense of reality? The Lord will make His point and He will have His way. Jonah saw this come to pass.

The Lord's reply to Jonah's outlandish comments was, *"You have been concerned about this plant, though you did not tend it or make it grow. It sprang up overnight and died overnight."* Didn't Jonah think that a plant growing large enough for shade overnight and then literally dying the next day was a little weird? That must have been some huge worm.

Here's the punchline of the whole story and the epitome of the Lord's care for people:

"Should I not have concern for the great city of Nineveh, in which there are more than a hundred and twenty thousand people who cannot tell their right hand from their left—and also many animals?" (Jonah 4:11 [NIV]).

I have heard it said that God steers the tiller of our lives and Jonah's life. It is not for us to get involved in all the details of His spinning. It's our responsibility to be still and confident as the storms rage on; He has a plan.

Like Jonah, I too once faced a storm and saw God's plan at work.

As a young child, I grew up sailing on Lake Michigan, a magnificent body of sky-blue crystal-clear water. My father was a master racer of sailboats. The big Queen's Cup Race was across Lake Michigan. Dad was a confident, competent sailor. When he was at the helm, no one worried. We always knew dad had everything under control. We faced some harrowing storms on that 80-mile-long lake.

When crossing the lake one summer during a spectacular thunderstorm in the middle of the night, my friend and I were in the cabin, braced down on the bow as the boat smashed the waves like a knife slicing butter. We braced our feet on one end of the bow and our heads on the other. The wind howled and the sails ruffled.

Our boat was heeling at a 90-degree angle from the gale force winds. Any further and we'd flip over. The rain pelted the hatch of our cabin like sleet on a window. The thunder cracked and lit up the entire cabin.

Yet I slept like a baby in the bow of our boat because to me, it was just a fun adventure—like a ride at Six Flags. Why? Because Dad was at the helm.

But this assurance of safety was not so for my friend, who was scared to death. She had no history with my dad's competence. She didn't know his sailing history or how he had faithfully cared for me. She had not been raised on boats and in storms with my dad.

As we grow in the knowledge of God in our lives, we gain confidence in His never-ending care and love no matter what we are experiencing.

Charles Spurgeon in his Morning and Evening, August 5 says it best:

"Every event as yet has worked out the most divinely blessed results. So, believing that God rules all, that he governs wisely, that he brings good out of evil, the believer's heart is assured, and he is enabled calmly to meet each trial as it comes."[20]

To quote A. W. Tozer, "With the goodness of God to desire our highest welfare, the wisdom of God to plan it, and the power of God to achieve it, what do we lack? Surely, we are the most favored of all creatures."[21]

Chapter Four

GOD'S MAGNIFICENT PLAN
WITH JOSEPH'S SUFFERING

Rejoice, for your suffering is not a surprise, but a plan.

Joseph in the Bible seemed content in all his circumstances, whether tending sheep or checking in on his brothers at his dad's request. He was super devoted, very committed to his family, and seemed comfortable in every situation, even sharing his unusual dreams with his clan.

We all wish for brothers and sisters who are open and free to share like that, don't we? As I look at the blueprint of Joseph's life, I realize that God pre-planned his every step. I can learn and grow in the knowledge of God from this godly man's life.

These lessons will bring encouragement more precious than silver or gold in hopeless situations, as scripture affirms.

Joseph dreamt one evening that his brothers and even his father bowed down to him. *"Joseph had a dream, and when he told it to his brothers, they hated him all the more. He said to them, 'Listen to this dream I had: we were binding sheaves of grain out in the field when suddenly my sheaf rose and stood upright, while your sheaves gathered around mine and bowed down to it'"* (Genesis 37:7 [NIV]).

There it is. In his dream, Joseph's dad and brothers bowed down to him. The brothers were not happy. In fact, they began to fume in anger. The father, Jacob, loved Joseph more than his other sons because he was born late in his life. Joseph was also the baby of the family and was the son of Rachel, the favorite of Jacob's two wives. Joseph was the child everyone catered to. He was the favorite child who could get away with murder. He was the privileged child.

Moms and Dads tend to be lax with their younger children. You know how it is; they raise the older children with diligence, reading all the right books, going to seminars, and giving just the right foods with perseverance and dedication. But with their last child or children, the caboose, there is all grace and mercy: "Whatever you want, honey."

Firstborns know this well. You'll hear them lament all day long about how they never got to do anything.

"His brothers said to him, 'Do you intend to reign over us? Will you actually rule us?' And they hated him even more because of his dream and what he had said" (Genesis 37:8 [NIV]).

Later in the story, Israel (Jacob), asked Joseph to check on his older siblings shepherding the family's flocks. *"Go and see if all is well with your brothers and with the flocks, and bring word back to me"* (Genesis 37:14 [NIV]).

Joseph, being the obedient son he was, obliged and searched for his siblings.

"So Joseph went after his brothers and found them near Dothan. But they saw him in the distance, and before he reached them. they plotted to kill him. 'Here comes that dreamer!' they said to each other, 'Come now, let's kill him and throw him into one of these cisterns and say that a ferocious animal devoured him. Then we'll see what comes of his dreams'" (Genesis 37:17-20 [NIV]).

What? Murder your brother? Over a dream?

The brothers wanted to do away with Joseph. Their jealousy burned at the sight of him. "Kill him" was the chant. They wanted to murder Joseph, an immature young man, possibly a little arrogant, who was just trying to please his father and have a relationship with his siblings. Joseph got hoodwinked and bullied.

Genesis 37:23-24 (NIV) tells us, *"So when Joseph came to his brothers, they stripped him of his special robe—the ornate robe he was wearing [which his father gave him]—and they took him and threw him into the cistern. Thankfully, the cistern was empty; there was no water in it."*

Imagine Joseph's shock when his brothers tried to kill him. What was going through this young boy's mind as he sat in horror at the bottom of a dark and dirty well with no possible way of escape? A certain death awaited him. Where was his God, the God Whom he grew up with, the God who always watched his back?

Favor with a Capital F

Starving to death was a real possibility for Joseph. I'm sure he cried out in horror.

Have you ever been in a situation where you were in complete darkness? I met a woman last night at our neighborhood Christmas party who was once stuck in a dark, black-as-night elevator for three hours alone after the World Trade Center was attacked on 9/11.

Today, she suffers from PTSD.

Maybe this is how Joseph felt. His family members brought this horror to him.

He had a lot of time to think while deep in that hole. It doesn't say for how long Joseph was in the hole or what he did while in it. Maybe he prayed, "God, please bring someone to save my life." Maybe he bargained with God, "If you save me, I will serve you all of my days."

Meanwhile, the brothers spoke with each other over the heinous crime they committed. Judah (we'll call him the least bad brother) negotiated with the others and said, *"Come, let's sell him to the Ishmaelites and not lay our hands on him; after all, he is our brother, our own flesh and blood"* (Genesis 37:27 [NIV]).

So the new plan became "We won't kill him, we'll sell him as a slave, all under the auspice of he's our flesh and blood." This plan seemed agreeable to the brothers, so they pulled him out of the well and sold him for twenty shekels of silver to the Ishmaelites who took him to Egypt.

Joseph was sold into slavery by God's sovereign hands through his evil brothers.

In Genesis 50:20 (NIV) Joseph spoke about this: *"You intended to harm me, but God intended it for good ... the saving of many lives."*

Later we will see God's good plan and what this statement meant to a starving world.

After Joseph was sold by his own brothers to traveling Ishmaelites, he was sold to a man named Potiphar, from Egypt (Genesis 37:36).

Potiphar was the captain of the guard under Pharaoh. As his personal servant, Joseph lived in his home.

"When his master saw that the Lord was with him and that the Lord gave him success in everything he did, Joseph found favor in his master's eyes and became his attendant. Potiphar put him in charge of his household, and he entrusted to his care everything he owned" (Genesis 39:2-5 [NIV]).

Only God could give a purchased slave command over his master's house.

"The blessing of the Lord was on everything Potiphar had, both in the house and in the field. So Potiphar left everything he had in Joseph's care; with Joseph in charge, he did not concern himself with anything except the food he ate" (Genesis 39:5b-6 [NIV]).

Wow! Now that's favor with a capital F.

Do you need to know today that the favor of God rests on you?

I have a story in my own life of when God gave me favor with a capital F.

The other day, John and I were talking about how odd it is that we are invited to every neighbor's social gathering in our community. We just heard how only a few selected guests were invited to the latest neighborhood party, and we were one of them.

We barely knew these people. In fact, we almost didn't go. Interestingly though, John and I prayed what I like to call a fleece prayer.

"Lord, if you want us to go, let us run into the couple and they ask us if we're coming."

I figured this would never happen, saying, "Well, that's off my plate, whew."

Later that day, we unexpectedly ran into them.

"What are the chances?"

"You guys are coming tonight, aren't you?"

"Absolutely," John replied.

We knew there was no way out. God had spoken. So we gussied up and walked down to the bustling home all lit up for festivities.

Our church has a mission statement: "Every man, woman, and child for the gospel where we live, work, and play."

John and I take that mission statement seriously. God does too, I guess. I know you want to know what happened, but I don't have any spectacular God moments to share yet. I say yet because God is always at work. By the way, we are not that wonderful. I believe it is the favor of God 100 percent. He's endearing us to these neighbors, or I should say, they are being endeared to us.

When the Story Gets Worse

God had granted Joseph favor, but his story was about to turn sour.

When Joseph was in charge of all of Potiphar's treasures and when he had been committed to the godly care of his master's affairs, that's when Potiphar's wife attempted to seduce him.

We have not been told of her character until this point.

Joseph flat-out refused her persistent advances and said, "Potiphar trusts me with his whole household and does not concern himself with anything. Why in the world would I do such a wicked thing against God to someone who's been so gracious to me?" (Genesis 39:7-10, my paraphrase).

Still, she pursued him day after day.

I wonder what Joseph prayed. Maybe he said, "God save me from this lustful woman."

Joseph continued to avoid her, but she became exceedingly angry at him for not giving into her demands. Fuming, she conjured up a malicious, factious story to her servants and claimed that Joseph tried to rape her. She even tore her clothes for special effect. When Potiphar returned and heard the news, he burned with anger and placed Joseph in the king's prison. He absolutely believed his wife over his slave.

When I read this passage I said, "This, God, was your sovereign plan? How could you put an innocent man into prison by the hands of a lying, luring wife? He had been nothing but obedient and righteous, Lord."

Did Joseph realize God was in this elaborate plan?

It's one thing to fall into sin and expect consequences, jail time, and heartache, but it's quite another thing to be completely innocent and to be thrown into prison for punishment.

Oftentimes, the afflictions of the Lord's loved ones are for the good of others. Joseph, for example, was permitted to be a slave and be in prison so that by his suffering at the hands of evil people we might see the glory of God through His special favor on Joseph.

This is a great benefit for you and me to know today. As Charles Spurgeon says of Lazarus's illness and death, "His affliction was 'for the glory of God.' Throughout these nineteen hundred years which have succeeded Lazarus' story, all believers have been getting good out of it, and we are all the better because he languished and died. The church and the world may derive immense advantage through the sorrows of good men: the careless may be awakened, the doubting may be convinced, the ungodly may be converted, the mourner may be comforted through our testimony in sickness; and if so, would we wish to avoid pain and weakness?"[22]

When My Story Went from Good to Bad

We will circle back to Joseph's story in a moment. Don't worry, we won't leave him in prison forever.

But I'd like to highlight a story from my own life that Joseph's story reminded me of.

I was given a very special gift from the Lord many years ago. John and I had fertility issues. If you have this burden, you know firsthand the pain it causes. I had poured out the prayer to God fervently: "Please have me get pregnant."

Miraculously He answered my prayer. The doctors were stunned. When I went in to have the ultrasound, I was already two months pregnant. I was considered high risk. The doctors monitored my child with weekly ultrasounds where I would spend time with our son, Jonathan.

What a delightful time. He would fascinate us by sucking his thumb or grabbing his toes. He'd even do flips. What a show-off! We'd laugh. One day our very sweet neighbors came to visit him at our sonogram appointment. Bob had all kinds of questions for the technician. He asked if that tiny thing he saw on the screen was Jonathan's heart. Our nurse enlarged the area for Bob. Mary and I rolled our eyes, endeared by his inquisitiveness.

The tech noticed something she wasn't sure of, so out of caution, she sent us to the big hospital for a special Doppler screening of Jonathan. Mary and Bob waited in the room provided.

I went in the Doppler room with what looked to be a team of doctors. By now, they had lowered the lights and begun. Because I have a science background, I could discern enough of their words to know that my situation was not good.

After the ultrasound, they escorted me into a hospital room. I waited for what seemed like an hour. I'm sure it was just a few minutes. I remember looking out the big window onto the front of the hospital. It was a gray, dreary day, void of any color, drained until it looked like pale, white-washed skin. That's how I was feeling.

An older gentleman came in and without any emotion told me my son's heart was defective and he would die without a heart transplant. At least, that's the way I heard it.

What, God? This was my miracle child, the one You gave me against all odds; that's the one that's going to die? No! No! No! It can't be true.

We found out Jonathan had a heart condition that was irreparable.

We were told he would live one day to two weeks after birth. He was born via C-section on the second day of June because we wanted to give him every opportunity at life. He was beautiful. He was the healthiest-looking baby in the NICU, yet he was the one that was going to die. My husband wrote this fantastic story through Jonathan's eyes.

From Jonathan's Eyes

From his eyes ...

The Life of Jonathan Jared Schmidler 9:00 a.m., Monday, June 3 – Friday, June 7, 9:55 a.m. Jesus said, "*Let the little children come to me, and do not hinder them, for the Kingdom of Heaven belongs to such as these*" (Matthew 19:14 [NIV]).

June 3 – PRELUDE:

Mom and Dad got up at 4:30 a.m. to get to the hospital by 6:00 a.m., so this story could unfold. I had no way of knowing that the place I had called home for 38 weeks would soon be invaded by a doctor. I could tell something was up because Mom felt awfully nervous, and Dad sounded uptight. I heard them say we were at Indiana University Hospital, and that they were both afraid and lonely. Then they saw David Berthold, our shepherding minister, in the hallway of the labor delivery area and a peace settled over both Mom and Dad. David came just at the right time, and the action was now getting close.

DAY 1 – June 3, 1991
8:48 a.m.

I was born breech by C-section, which was a huge shock for me and lots of pain for Mom. Dad watched the whole time. The first guy I saw was Dr. Deaton, who I had heard many times, and it was great to associate a name with a face, even if I was upside down. He did a wonderful job with Mom and had to really work hard to get her back together. As they whisked me out of the operating room, the mood was all tense and professional—definitely all business.

Everyone was worried I might not make it, so they had a whole staff of doctors and nurses working on me to wake me up. At 8:47, I was in a warm, comfortable womb, and by 8:49, I was on a table under lights with doctors trying to convince me to breathe. Well, they succeeded because my work here on earth would not be done until Friday. And, besides, I had not met my Mom yet. When I woke up, Dad—wearing a goofy hat and mask—was staring at me. Dad then left to check on Mom and I met two special people who would be my friends my whole life; Dr. David Hertz and my nurse, Caryn Truelove.

Dad came back and said Mom was doing really well; she hoped that I was 4.5 pounds—but, to her amazement, I was only 7 lbs. 7 oz. and 20-1/2 inches long.

Once they stabilized me, it was time for the big moment—I got to meet my Mom. She was more beautiful than I ever expected, and now I know why I heard all those whistles (at least the first four months).

I could now see the love in her eyes, as well as feel it in my heart.

Because everyone was concerned about my heart, the doctors felt it best to take me over to Riley Children's Hospital, which specializes in children with severe health problems. They typically would put me in a metal container for the trip, but Dr. Hertz and Caryn pulled some strings and let Dad hold me while they pushed me in a wheelchair. Caryn pushed, Dr. Hertz directed; what a team—look out, Indy 500 fans.

The nursery in Module 5 at Riley would be my home for tonight. My nurse was Sabine Krueger (she told me how her first name was of German origin and pronounced Sah-BEAN-ah). She took great care of me on Monday. Dad was there the whole time. I think he forgot about Mom for a while. Sabine hooked me up to a heart and respiration monitor so they could keep track of me. I would set off the alarms on both units if anyone even tried to change my diaper. Dr. Darragh (my heart specialist) showed up at about 11:00 with his ultrasound machine to check my heart. He felt I would have a tough time using my heart for a very long time because all the parts weren't in the right places. It happened during the time I was developing, but it in no way affected the room I had available for love.

Mom got wheeled over on her bed, and it was good to see her ... I missed her. I'm so glad Michelle, Julie, Debbie, and Kim were with Mom, because I think Dad forgot about her. Next, I saw Grandma and Grandpa Nigel and Aunt Barbara. I was as excited to see them as they were to see me. It's great to have grandparents.

They all held and rocked me ... it was great.

Mom stayed until 4:30 and then got wheeled back to I.U. She was tired.

Lots of Mom and Dad's friends came to visit Mom at I.U.; Dad escorted each one to see me—he was truly a proud Daddy. Even more of their friends called to check up on us; it was great. I slept at Riley tonight, mostly in Sabine's arms. She said I was a model patient.

It was a good day ...

DAY 2 – June 4, 1991

I woke up early and Sabine was rocking me, attempting to get me to eat some awful-tasting formula. I showed her. Mom and Dad came over early ... Mom was still in her bed.

As I looked around the Intensive Care Unit, I saw all kinds of children who needed lots of help. I hope they all make it. I really didn't look like I should be there because my appearance on the outside was great—it was inside where the problems were. The doctors felt I wouldn't make it very long, but I'd show them.

I had many visitors today, all friends of Mom and Dad ... and now of me. It was great to meet them and have them hold me.

Grandma and Grandpa Schmidler got here at 12:00 noon. It was exciting to meet them. It's great to have grandparents.

The doctors stopped giving me the medication which was supposed to help my heart at 1:30 p.m. They felt I would be in trouble without it, but I actually did better ... I think it has to do with determined parents.

Neil Norheim (Mom and Dad's minister) came to see me next.

He was a big help to Mom and Dad and gave them strength when they needed it most. He prayed a wonderful prayer for me and my family, and it really helped us.

It was then time for us to be a family, so Mom, Dad and I set out for I.U. Hospital. Aunt Michelle somehow arranged to get us a suite at I.U. They said it was not possible, but my Aunt Michelle is very determined.

On the way, we stopped at the chapel so I could get baptized, not because I felt I had to, but because the grandparents thought it was a good idea. So, even though Mom and Dad knew I was sinless and would go to Heaven, they baptized me out of love for my grandmas and grandpas. Neil prayed again, and there wasn't a dry cheek in the chapel.

Jane Garrido brought me my first toy, a beautiful Teddy Bear with a rattle. It was fun to play with.

We got to our room at I.U. and it was perfect ... nice and private and big.

The first thing Mom did was nap while Dad and I watched cartoons. I prefer "Looney Toons."

We had lots of visitors tonight—all wonderful friends of Mom and Dad from church, work, neighbors; they all made me feel so loved. It is nice to have so many new friends. Even more of them called and left notes. It's really great to be so popular.

Uncle Phil McCauley brought in his video camera to take some pictures, even though Dad didn't think it was a great idea. As it turned out, Dad cherishes this tape more than anything ... I guess it goes to show that even the best Dad is human.

Day 2 – Night

Dad and I watched a basketball game tonight. It was an NBA finals game. Chicago won ...

Dad slept.

We were all lying in bed, ready for sleep and Dad was just about ready to call the nursery and have them get me. That's when Aunt Terri McCauley called Dad (11:15 p.m.) to see what was up. Dad told her he was going to put me in the nursery, and Aunt Terri said, "NO WAY"—she said I needed to be held at all times by loving friends and family. Dad couldn't agree more, so he told the nurses to keep checking on us—which they did so well. Aunt Terri arrived at 1:30 a.m. to relieve Dad because he was tired. She read me nursery rhymes and held and rocked me. I could tell she had lots of experience being a mom.

It was a good day ...

DAY 3 – June 5, 1991

It was a family day for me. I was spending the whole day with Mom and Dad at I.U. Grandma and Grandpa Nigel came to visit me in the morning and brought Aunt Barbara along. I love seeing relatives! They held me for a long time ... Grandma did the most holding. It was a fun morning.

Dad took me outside to see the world at 11:30 a.m. He felt I needed some fresh air, and he probably did too. We walked over to Arby's to get Mom a shake ... chocolate, of course. I got to see the sun (which my eyes didn't like at first, but they got used to it) and the bluest sky ever. We watched a guy cut grass and smelled that fresh smell. I saw trees, a bird, clouds, and a semi (which let me know what diesel fuel smells like). It was a perfect day to be alive. We delivered the shake to Mom, as requested.

Grandma and Grandpa Schmidler came in the afternoon, and it was so good to see them again. They held me a long time ... Grandma did most of the holding. It was a fun afternoon. We spent the night as a threesome, with Mom doing most of the holding and always trying to push a bottle in my mouth. I guess she didn't realize I can't power eat like her and Dad.

About 2:00 a.m. I wasn't doing too well ... in fact, Mom and Dad didn't think I would make it much longer. They made a big tearful fuss and said all kinds of goodbyes, thinking I was going somewhere. Quite frankly, the only place I was going was into Dr. Hertz's arms as he carried me out of the room and rocked me in a rocking chair for hours. Then about 4:00 a.m., my friend Nurse

Caryn called to check on me, and when she heard I wasn't doing so well, she rushed in. She found me in Dr. Hertz's arms, both of us sound asleep. Mom and Dad needed some relief, so she took care of me the rest of the day (it was a long day for her).

Mom and Dad fell asleep waiting for the news, but later, when Dad called at 5:30 a.m., I could hear his relief, and Caryn brought me back to Mom and Dad's room.

It was a good day ...

DAY 4 – June 6, 1991

It was another beautiful day ... as expected.

Today was another family day ... just Mom, Dad and me.

Dad got a wheelchair and pushed Mom and me outside. We went for a long walk, and I got to see Dad's driving firsthand (WOW!).

We went to a park, and I saw birds, bushes, a hill, picnic tables, park benches, sidewalks made of brick, a statue, and experienced all kinds of great smells. I could tell it was making Mom and Dad feel lots better, especially since I had my big blue eyes open the whole trip. People came by and said I was so cute. I thought handsome was more appropriate, but I'd settled for cute at 79 hours old.

On our way back, I saw a Ferrari get a parking ticket ... Dad said the owner could afford it.

It was a great day with Mom and Dad—they are special.

I needed some help tonight because I was not very comfortable, but Caryn and Donna took care of it right away. I spent the whole night sleeping in the bed between Mom and Dad. Dad was so happy and thankful Caryn got him a bed ... I think he actually slept.

It was a good day ...

DAY 5 – June 7, 1991

It was another beautiful day ... a perfect day to go to Heaven.

Dad got Mom going early and the three of us went for another walk—well, Dad walked ...

Mom and I rode in the wheelchair.

We went back to the park and I got to go on a swing (with Dad) and a merry-go-round with Mom and Dad. We were having a great time, and my eyes were open wide the whole time.

About 9:00, we headed back to our room. Dad showed me how to run on the way back as he pushed the wheelchair at full speed. It was fun.

By the time I got back to the room, I wasn't feeling too good, but I still had no pain. Mom worried about that all the time, but thanks to her, I never felt pain at all. Dad took me from Mom's arms and I looked at her and said, "I love you." Dad carried me to Caryn's office to have her check me over.

At 9:55 a.m., I looked up and saw Heaven ... it was beautiful. I took one last look at Dad and one final thought of Mom—the best parents any kid could hope for. But my view of Heaven was too intriguing, and when Jesus called my name and asked me to follow him, I felt it was my time to go.

I know I left some hurting hearts behind, but that's the way God planned it. Because each of you that hurts does so because of your love for my Mom and Dad and their family. Each kind thing you did, each prayer, each special card, each flower, and each warm thought from you took a small slice of pain from my family's heart and replaced it with love. That's why you hurt now, so be thankful for it because your kindness and love earned it.

Soon that pain will again transform to love and allow us all to carry on and help us all find the way that will ensure we all meet in Heaven someday.

I love you, Mommy ... I love you, Daddy ... I love you, Grandmas ... I love you Grandpas.

I love all of you friends that I met and those I didn't ... because if you have read this, you have touched my family's lives. Thank you so much for that.

Love,

Jonathan

It was a good day ...

To Jonathan Jared Schmidler

God sent our precious jewel for a few brief days to dwell among His children here on earth, His love alone to tell. Jonathan, your life held meaning. Though your life was so brief, your birth and your time on earth impacted friends, family, and even strangers.

Your coming and your going brought joy and pain together to pave the road we all must take with love that lasts forever!

We know now God has blessed us with a son to love and to share. Our precious jewel has returned to His own loving care.

Iris M. Marshall, (a dear family friend).

God had a plan for Jonathan's short life and for us too. Life didn't look the way we'd hoped. It didn't feel fair, either. But God was with all of us from the beginning to the end. God never, not for one moment, left us alone. He comforted us, encouraged us and gave us hope to our shattered hearts. He does promise, you know.

Isaiah 49:23b (NIV) says, "Those who hope in me will not be disappointed."

Joseph in Prison

As promised, we're circling back to Joseph.

The Lord was with Joseph in that prison; He showed him kindness and granted him favor in the eyes of the prison warden.

Genesis 39:22 (NIV) says, *"So the warden put Joseph in charge of all those held in prison, and he was made responsible for all that was done there."*

The warden paid no attention to anything under Joseph's care, because the Lord was with Joseph and gave him success in whatever he did."

Joseph did not receive deliverance from undeserved circumstances as we so often hope for. Instead, he received favor. This begs the question ...

"Lord, if we do what's right, shouldn't we expect favorable treatment?"

Joseph flourished in whatever situations God placed him in. He must have figured he'd do his best job and be a blessing wherever he was placed. Oh, that I could have those conscious ethics in my conduct. Joseph demonstrated sacrificial grace against all unfairness. He didn't demand rights. No. He humbly accepted his circumstances from God, knowing full well He was in charge.

"To actively [with our actions] believe that our Heavenly Father constantly spreads around us providential circumstances that work for our present good and our everlasting well-being brings to the soul a veritable benediction."[23]

God accepts full responsibility for His actions. Let's not relieve God as King over the universe by trying to control what His responsibility is.

Joseph obeyed God with complete obedience. So did Abraham, when called to put his one and only son, Isaac, on the altar to be sacrificed. In complete obedience, he did as the Lord commanded, knowing full well God had a supreme plan that He would deliver with flawless precision.

Even if it meant Abraham's own son's death. That's faith.

For sure and certain, God won't let us down. I was sure and certain when my son was diagnosed with a fatal heart condition, and He got me all the way through that tragedy.

Faith is pressing into the hard thing and trusting it's going to be okay because God is on the throne. We don't run, though every bone in our body wants to. We grab hold of the tree of life with all our strength even though everything looks like it is going to hell in a handbasket.

Hebrews 11:19 tells us that Abraham reasoned that if Isaac died, God would be able to bring him back to life again. In a sense, Abraham did receive his son back from the dead.

God, at the last second, supplied a ram substitute. The knife was literally coming down when the angel told Abraham, "Stop."

Why, why, why, does God always wait till the very last second to deliver me from my problems? It always feels way too late.

I suffer so much trauma, anxiety, and fear before He arrives.

Sisters Mary and Martha likely experienced this as well when their brother passed away. They'd felt God had come too late. When Lazarus died, Jesus said, *"I am glad I was not there, so that you may believe"* (John 11:15 [NIV]).

He let Lazarus die. He was dead for four days. Yet, He did this so that we could see Him raise Lazarus from the dead. How much more will we believe when we are in excruciatingly hard situations and God delivers us? Wait patiently, friends. God's always working on our behalf, moving pieces, making plans, delivering souls, and speaking life.

I have so much farther to climb on this journey of accepting my heavenly Father's good plans for my life. How about you? I want to learn from Joseph's surrendered attitude while suffering at the hands of unjust, undeserved treatment.

When your goodness is evilly spoken of, when your wishes are crossed, your advice disregarded, your opinions ridiculed, and you refuse to let any anger rise in your heart or even defend yourself but instead endure everything in patient, loving silence ...

That's Joseph.

Meanwhile, in Prison ...

The king's cupbearer and chief baker were thrown into prison under Joseph's care. The two men had dreams and went to Joseph to interpret them. The cupbearer's dream ended favorably, and he was restored to his position, while the chief baker's dream ended very badly and he was killed. Both of Joseph's interpretations of the dreams came to be true. Joseph asked the cupbearer if he would remind Pharaoh to get him out of prison. *"I was put here falsely"* he said (Genesis 40:15, my paraphrase).

Way to stand up for yourself, Joseph. It's about time, I thought.

"'Happily, I will,' the cupbearer said. The chief cupbearer, however, did not remember Joseph; he forgot him" (Genesis 40:15, 23, my paraphrase).

What? How in the world, after such a traumatic event of dreams, could the cupbearer forget! Impossible. Only God! *Why, Lord, would you have this poor man stay in prison so long?*

God turns things upside down (Isaiah 29:16).

How devastating this must have been for Joseph, who stayed in prison for another two years.

But God was still working in Joseph's life. God is the same yesterday, today, and forever. He's working in our lives in the same way. We cannot let discouragement overwhelm us. I want to strive to be a thriver, not just a survivor in my dark times.

How? By resting confidently in the One Who knows all my woes.

Soon we will see all God was doing behind the upside down scenes in Joseph's life.

God, Bringing it All Together

After Joseph had been in prison for an extended two years due to the cupbearer's absent-mindedness, Pharaoh started experiencing troubling dreams that his magicians could not decipher. Finally, the cupbearer came to his senses and remembered that Joseph could interpret dreams.

All quotes in this section will be taken from Genesis 41.

"Pharaoh said to Joseph, 'I had a dream, and no one can interpret it. But I have heard it said of you that when you hear a dream you can interpret it'" (Genesis 41:1 [NIV]).

"'I cannot do it,' Joseph replied to Pharaoh, 'but God will give Pharaoh the answer he desires.' ... God has revealed to Pharoh what he is about to do.'" (Genesis 41:16, 25 [NIV]).

Joseph continued speaking to Pharoah. *"It is just as I said to Pharaoh: God has shown Pharaoh what he is about to do. Seven years of great abundance are coming throughout the land of Egypt, but seven years of famine will follow them. Then all the abundance in Egypt will be forgotten, and the famine will ravage the land. The abundance in the land will not be remembered, because the famine that follows it will be so severe"* (Genesis 41:28-31 [NIV]).

There were quite a few years of difficulty ahead for Egypt as well as for the rest of the known world at that time.

God gave Joseph a master blueprint for the worldwide famine that was coming. He put a wise and discerning man in charge of the land of Egypt.

So Joseph told him a plan to prepare for the famine. *"Let Pharaoh appoint commissioners over the land to take a fifth of the harvest of Egypt during the seven years of abundance ... to be kept in the cities for food. This food should be held in reserve for the country, to be used during the seven years of famine that will come upon Egypt, so that the country may not be ruined by the famine"* (Genesis 41:34-36 [NIV]).

The plan seemed good to Pharaoh so he asked, *"Can we find anyone like this man, one whom is the spirit of God?'"* (Genesis 41:38 [NIV]).

Next, we find out the whole reason for Joseph's life, the preplanned circumstances for His purpose on this earth. Let's watch it unfold:

"Then Pharaoh said to Joseph, 'Since God has made all this known to you, [this special blueprint] there is no one so discerning and wise as you. You shall be in charge of my palace, and all my people are to submit to your orders. Only with respect to the throne will I be greater than you'" (Genesis 41:39-40 [NIV]).

Let's recap on Joseph's life. His brothers attempted to murder him by throwing him down a well to die, only to pull him back out and sell him as a slave to Egypt. He is then falsely accused of rape by his master's wife and unjustly thrown into prison.

He's unnoticed in prison and spends two extra years there.

After all that torture and trauma on earth, he gets exalted to number two, only under the king, Pharaoh.

That's God's upside down way.

What a life. Now, if God would have told him the plan ahead of time, I wonder what he would have said. "Send someone else or maybe someone much more righteous, whatever you want, Lord."

I'm so glad God doesn't give me my blueprint ahead of time. A possible terminal cancer at twenty-five. The loss of a child at thirty-four. More cancer later. The list is long. I'm so grateful for it all today because God has revealed Himself and His plans as much as I can know. He's proven Himself worthy to handle all my troubles. It's not that He must do it, but He does it anyway. Oh, how He loves you and me.

Irony in Joseph's Story

Remember the tell-all dream Joseph had about his brothers bowing down to him? Well, get ready.

"So Pharaoh said to Joseph, 'I hereby put you in charge of the whole land of Egypt … No one will lift a hand or foot without your word'" (Genesis 41:41, 44, my paraphrase).

Pharaoh gave Joseph a wife, and he had two children. One of them he named Manasseh because he said, "*It is because God has made me forget all my trouble and all my father's household*" (Vs. 51). This is the first time we hear of Joseph express heartache over all his past misery.

The second child was named Ephraim, "*because God had made me fruitful in the land of my suffering*" (Genesis 41:52 [NIV]).

The famine hit just as God said it would. "*All the world came to Egypt to buy grain from Joseph, because the famine was so severe everywhere*" (Genesis 41:57 [NIV]). The entire world was coming to Joseph. That's a lot to take in from a boy who was once thrown into a well.

Meanwhile, Joseph's father sent his brothers to Egypt to buy food because the whole world was starving. When they arrived, they bowed down to Joseph with all their faces to the ground.

Although Joseph recognized them, they did not recognize him, and he remembered his dream about them.

God's Plan Coming to Fruition

Joseph revealed himself to his brothers.

Genesis 45:4-8 (NIV) tells us:

"Then Joseph said to his brothers, 'Come close to me.' When they had done so, he said, 'I am your brother Joseph, the one you sold into Egypt! And now, do not be distressed and do not be angry with yourselves for selling me here, because it was to save lives that God sent me ahead of you. For two years now there has been famine in the land, and for the next five years there will be no plowing and reaping. But God sent me ahead of you to preserve for you a remnant on earth and to save your lives by a great deliverance.

So then, it was not you who sent me here, but God. He made me father to Pharaoh, lord of his entire household and ruler of all Egypt.'"

Let's note what is being said.

1. I'm Joseph, the one you sold into Egypt.

2. It was to save lives that I was sold into slavery by your hands. God sent me.

3. God sent me to preserve for you a remnant on earth and to save your lives!

4. It was not you who sent me here but God. (Not your evilness against me, brothers.)

5. He made me ruler of all of Egypt.

Joseph reminds us all in Genesis 50:20 (NIV), *"You intended to harm me, but God intended it for good to accomplish what is now being done, the saving of many lives."*

Joseph's life was predetermined by God for His good purposes.

Psalm 139:16 (my paraphrase) says, *"Your life and mine are also predetermined. It's written in God's book. Every hour of every day is already written in God's book."*

Ephesians 2:10 (NIV) states, *"We are God's handiwork, created in Christ Jesus to do good works, which God prepared in advance for us to do."*

Our Dear Friend's Story

When I think of Joseph's story, I think of this.

Our friend Nick said to his lovely wife, Mary, "All our dreams for ministering in the Middle East are coming true. I love America. After all, I'm as American as apple pie. But my heart is in the Middle East as I know yours is." They, newly married in the States, had been planning for many years to return to what they called home. Both sets of their parents were doctors in the Middle East. Nick and Mary fell in love in the Middle East. That's where they'd both been to boarding school, and all their life's milestones had happened in the Middle East.

Today Nick runs the mission's group at our midwestern church in the USA with a confidence that makes you want to go on every mission's journey alongside him.

He has a zest for life that compels even the timid traveler to experience his journeys. He can sell popsicles to Inuit people or make you desire Saudi Arabia in the middle of a 120-degree summer. Believe me, he goes to the rarest corners of our planet too. I know it's God's calling and equipping in his life. It is the Holy Spirit working on both ends, deliverer and hearer, to get us all excited about missions.

Even Nick's zest is from God. Nick is like a father who holds you and says, "This is going to be a thrill, but you have to trust me." He's that kind of dad. He leads with grace and precision. His winsome words, like a finely tuned harp, attract both contemplating visitors and those considering a life-changing journey.

John and I were drawn to this couple immediately. Nick is a cut-up, risk-taking adventurer. Mary is creative, artistic, and warmly inviting by nature. She can whip up a precise and gorgeously decorated accent pillow in a quick second. Mary is sensitive and compassionate.

No thought is left unturned with Mary. Spending time with her makes you feel like you've had a warm cup of tea on a cold day. Her calming spirit soothes all those nearest to her. When you're with Mary, you had better take your shoes off and put your feet up because you're going to have a massage on your soul. When we're together, we share the deepest things on our hearts, the kinds of things said around a home-cooked meal with closest friends.

Can you see God's wisdom in bringing this couple together for rough, rugged ends-of-the-earth mission journeys as well as other adventures?

How God intersected their story is quite phenomenal and inspirational, and their union is a match made in heaven.

Nick and Mary were married in the USA, and shortly after they realized God was calling them back to their Middle Eastern home. Although raising three children in a third-world country would be extremely taxing, their goal was to build a seminary where pastors could be trained to minister to people. Unfortunately, God did not provide the funds they needed, so they plodded along many years with purchased land and no provision for the very thing God had put on their hearts.

Imagine being in a communist country with no family, few friends, and extraordinarily hard work, while desperately hanging onto what you believe is God's purpose for your life. I'd be saying, "Lord, did I hear you? Why are you not providing? You provided for Nehemiah when he was called to build the wall."

All this heartache overwhelmed Mary, who was raising three young children with little provision and less helping hands.

You may know what it is like to have family and friends come alongside you when your children are young. Now put yourself in a foreign, third-world country. Even a gallon of milk and breakfast cereal is hard to come by, and there is no TV to occupy your kids with during their monster hours. Heaven forbid there is an iPad with games and videos to entertain them.

Mary became clinically depressed. She fought these demons as hard as she could, literally year after year. Both Mary's and Nick's parents were missionaries; to them, this was what you did. After all, it was God's calling. You should be willing to sacrifice yourself for the cause.

Hard as she tried, Mary's depression only got worse. Good, faithful church people wanted to help her. "Mary, you just need more faith."

Sounds familiar, doesn't it?

Joseph and Mary had hard circumstances, and so did a man named Job.

We will learn from Job's friends in Job 8. Job lost his children, relatives, brothers, sisters, cattle, and servants. He was left with a terrible disease of scabs and boils on his skin. His friends told him, *"But if you will seek God earnestly and plead with the Almighty, if you are pure and upright, even now he will rouse himself on your behalf and restore you ..."* (Job 8:5-6 [NIV]).

We find out God had a very different plan for Job.

Sometimes there are godly, well-meaning people who just don't understand you. Because they want relief for you as their friend, they say things that are simply not true, just like Job's friends did.

There's a lesson here for me when I think back to the story of Mary.

In God's providence, Mary kept getting worse. Deep darkness took over her, crippling her as well as her entire family. What could Nick do? The overseers of his ministry needed to know about Mary's condition. Nick knew Mary needed more help than was available in the rural country they were living in. Their ministry decided to bring them back to America.

How devastating it must have been for Mary and Nick to have their dreams dashed to smithereens. But God had other plans working, just like He did in Joseph's life.

Imagine God calling you to a very difficult, foreign country for years of hard living and persevering in your work for an expected goal.

As 1 Corinthians 9:24-5 (NIV) states, *"Do you not know that in a race all the runners run, but only one gets the prize? Run in such a way as to get the prize. Everyone who competes in the games goes into strict training. They do it to get a crown that will not last, but we do it to get a crown that will last forever."*

Nick and Mary had been running as runners in a race for a prize. Then the thing they'd been burdened to do was smashed, failed, discontinued, and disintegrated. No seminary! How completely life shattered they must have felt. Did God let them down? Heavens no!

Arriving back in the States, Mary received the much-needed, life-saving help she needed and she began to heal. Their children settled into American life. Meanwhile, Nick looked for a job. They had left the mission field. What else could they do?

But God says His plans for us will never be thwarted.

A large Midwestern church decided to hire Nick in their mission's department.

This reminds me of Proverbs 16:9 (my paraphrase): *"We make our plans, but the Lord determines our steps."*

This was a perfect position for Nick, whose burden from God was for missions around the world. This was a match made in heaven. He could now support all the countries he felt a burden for by bringing the gospel to them through this great, reliable platform. "Every nation under God" became his motto.

Talk about an instant expansion of your calling.

Seriously, God, from Mary's depression?

Here's the exciting part. This particular midwestern church gives a special Christmas offering to different missions each year.

The lead pastor asked Nick if they could use the Christmas offering that year to build a seminary in his home country, his missionary land.

What?! This was exactly what Nick spent all those years back home trying to accomplish. The offering had to be approved by the congregation. Can you guess what they said? Yes! The church gave far above and beyond what was needed, nearly a million dollars.

This was not news to God, it was all scripted in heaven.

A Necessary Recap

Mary was afflicted with a very serious depression, so she and her family had to leave the Middle East and return to America. This was so Nick could work at this particular church which he did not even seek out, so all the givers in the congregation could be blessed to participate in the Lord's work in giving to what God had called Nick and Mary to do. It was a God-sized project. The plan was brilliant since there had previously been no possible way to raise the money needed for the work in the Middle East.

As we recap Mary's story, I am reminded of the prophet Nehemiah.

Nehemiah had a similar problem with rebuilding the wall. Grieved over the wall of Jerusalem being broken down, God gave Nehemiah favor to go and rebuild it. It was a monumental task. Nehemiah had to trust God for the next step. God had to provide the funds and the people needed to build the structure.

Do you know God moved the people's hearts to give finances to the rebuilding? They gave out of their hearts. Amazing!

Proverbs 21:1 says *"The King's heart is in the hands of the Lord, like the rivers of water He turns it wherever He wishes"* (my NIV paraphrase).

That's what happened with my dear friends Nick and Mary. God's plans happened.

His work will never be thwarted, not because of lack of funds, enemies, natural disasters, or anything else.

Job 42:2 (NIV) says, *"I know that you can do all things; no purpose of yours can be thwarted."*

Nick and Mary have been overjoyed to see God's work on their behalf in and through their tragedy. In the Bible and outside of it, God always has a great purpose, future, and hope for His people.

Jeremiah 29:11 (NIV) reminds us, *"'For I know the plans I have for you,' declares the Lord, 'plans to prosper you and not to harm you, plans to give you a hope and a future."*

Romans 15:13 puts it perfectly, *"May the God of hope fill you with all joy and peace as you trust in him, so that you may overflow with hope by the power of the Holy Spirit."*

This story taught me God is intimately involved in all the details of my life, the good ones and the bad ones. It is all for His grand purpose of ultimate greatness. His purposes and His ways are always just, right, and perfect.

"He is the Rock, his works are perfect, and all his ways are just. A faithful God who does no wrong, upright and just is he" (Deuteronomy 32:4 [NIV]).

When things get hard, I'm learning to bow my head and proclaim to myself, "Yes, Lord, Your ways are perfect. I put my head down and remind myself of Your grand purpose, one too wonderful for me to know."

Psalm 139:14 (NIV) reminds me, *"I praise you because I am fearfully and wonderfully made; your works are wonderful, I know that full well."*

It can often feel like we're looking at the back of a tapestry, instead of the front. So I pray, "Lord, help me to see through Your eyes the front side of the tapestry when the gnarly, knotted back is all that's looming in front of me."

Staying Focused

Joseph learned to keep focused on God while He worked through every evil thing done to him.

Instead of looking at the wrong done, he looked to God, Who was over all of it. This changed everything.

He could no longer be bitter, jealous, vindictive, or retaliatory.

Imagine adopting such a mindset that changes your plans, thoughts, and perspective. All the endless misery, negativity in your mind, and all the records of the wrongs people have done to you would leave!

Joseph didn't ignore the things done against him, he just refused to let himself be controlled by that narrative.

We tend to act on how we feel, so change the feelings of "poor me" to "all that's been done to me helps my faith." God has got our future in His hands.

Joseph kept his focus and look where his life ended up. Each trial built him up for the next adventure God had for him.

Joseph did not let his pain get in the way of his decisions. He stayed laser-focused on the truth.

All things fall in the sovereignty of God. Even sinful men's ways are in His saving purposes. For example, although Joseph's brothers and Potiphar's wife treated him poorly, God worked this together for His good.

Joseph had plenty of unfair stuff happen to him. Imagine if he lived daily saying, "My brothers threw me in a well to die," or "I was put in prison for something I didn't do." If he played the hopeless reel, it would have chained him to misery. He would have given away his supernatural power from God for accomplishing His will. He would not have been second in command in Egypt. He would not have delivered people from starvation. Wow! How awful that would have been for him.

Note to self: The hopeless reel we play of bad things in our lives can turn into bitterness.

Although Joseph's brothers hurt him, he realized God used that very thing for His good purpose. Joseph moved on to forgiveness. He gave the seven times seven forgiveness that Jesus talks about. He extended the every minute of everyday kind of forgiveness that God asks us to live in.

We think of Joseph as a victim, but his father called him *"a fruitful vine near a spring, whose branches climb over a wall"* (Genesis 49:22 [NIV]).

This was after all his troubles. Joseph chose better over bitter. He chose to focus on what God was doing rather than focusing on what he'd been through. He focused on how he would get over things instead of focusing on what stood against him. He was not chained down by the way things went down. He believed he had to climb over the wall or die on the wall. He must have realized he could not climb over his trouble if he complained.

It's a fight to stay accurately focused and to believe the truth enough to keep God at the center of your problems.

His father Jacob said, *"With bitterness archers attacked him, they shot him with hostility. But his bow remained steady, his strong arms stayed limber, because of the hand of the mighty one of Jacob"* (Genesis 49:23 [NIV]).

Amazingly, through all his pain, Joseph never lost his focus.

Note to myself: Keep laser-focused on God so I can climb over my problems. Never get stuck in the quicksand of "I've been wronged. It's not fair. Others have it better than me. I'm a poor, pitiful victim."

With emphasis on *pit*iful—Lord—keep me far from that pit.

God's Ultimate Purpose

We can't leave before taking in another succulent morsel from Joseph's story.

Check out what happens in Genesis 45:14-15. Joseph threw his arms around his brothers, kissed them, and wept over them! Yes, the same brothers who tried to kill him and sold him into slavery. Wow. He hugged and kissed each one of them.

No one was left aside, and no one came to apologize, "I'm so sorry for trying to knock you off." All this forgiveness granted was one-sided. After Joseph's grand spectacle of love, the brothers talked with him.

A total restoration came into Joseph's family all because of his willingness to give up all his rights for the higher cause of God's will.

I can't even imagine what the brothers were feeling right then. They were given the prime fat of the land in Egypt to live on while in the midst of a seven-year famine. Was this a reward? It certainly was not deserved. They knew that well in their hearts.

Is this what it looks like to love those who often feel like enemies? This forgiveness reminds me of a story. The son-in-law of my dear friend Angela's only daughter was having an affair. Angela deducted this from a woman being at the family's house way too often. At the time, Angela's daughter was suffering from addictions and had abandoned her family.

During Christmas, Angela was visiting her granddaughter and their family when up drove her son-in-law with the suspected woman. So many fleeting thoughts ran through Angela's mind.

"How could he? How could she come here?" The pain was excruciating.

"Where can I run to escape this nightmare? Should we even get out of the car, Bob?"

Meanwhile, the son-in-law and woman got out of the car.

It was Angela's daughter's best friend. The family and Angela knew her well. She had been to many family functions.

Well, Angela knew something needed to happen soon or it would get more awkward and suspicious than it already was. Hesitantly, Angela opened her car door, "Now or never."

Despite her shattered heart, she prayed to God, "Please help."

As she walked up to the adulterers, something amazing happened. Angela threw her arms around this woman and gave her a big hug. Angela knew her well as her daughter's best friend.

What a chaotic mess my friend was thrown in the middle of.

Many of us live in disfunction we never created. This is what happens when our focus is on God, not the adulterous mess.

God had an ultimate purpose in Joseph's misery and his brothers' evilness against him. This was true for Angela's family and our families too.

The Ball Is in Our Court

I wonder what would happen if, beginning with our hearts, we surrendered to what God wants, even when no one apologizes to us.

Today, the ball is in our court.

With God on our side, who can be against us? There's only one thing to do. **Step off the comfortable ledge** to the unknown below.

It's all very scary when we look at the ledge and below and then back to the safe comfort behind us. But that "safe" view is fictitious. The real view is in the leap ahead.

When I think of making that leap, I think of a party I recently attended. A man shared his difficult past and how he had a deadbeat dad who was not around for his growing up years.

Have you ever heard a story like that before? He tried to close the gap with a phone call, but there was no response. Despite the outcome, I'm proud that he took initiative and did the hardest thing—he stepped into the hard.

We are not responsible for outcomes. God is, and we can hold Him to that.

I know this man will not be disappointed because he did the hard thing. Actions like these allow us to sleep at night, while our unmade actions keep us tossing.

We could have a similar story at any party we attend.

Joseph kept his eye on the prize, and everyone, including himself, was blessed.

It's a complete work of God in just the asking. Let's not ask God to change the people who hurt us. Let's ask God to change us.

What if you were the vessel of change in the family?

I wonder what world we'd be saving if we were all self-sacrificing? I mean the go low, humble yourself on the altar of your rights for the greater good kind of self-sacrifice.

You say, "But you don't know what they did to me." So many of those responses I cannot understand. I've not been in your shoes and you've not been in mine, but Joseph has and so has Jesus.

Jesus has been through more than your hardest attack.

Talk yourself into the long view, the end goal, the outcome. Write down your hope and future. Ask God to give you the desires of His heart and of your heart. Then step off the ledge into the hard. Exhilarate yourself. God's plans are not predictable, but they are completely right.

Questions

1. Now that you know the truth, God is in the center of your mess, how will this knowledge affect your present circumstances?

2. Where do you need God's peaceful reminder that He's in control of your life?

3. Who can you share this knowledge with today? How could that help them succeed and be content?

4. The Lord wants us to be free to delight. What chains of lies might you be clinging to?

5. How can we be more like Joseph and have patience without grumbling?

6. Write a sentence of help you can bring with you to put God in the center of it all.

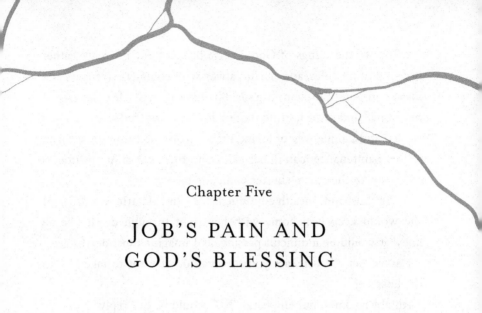

Chapter Five

JOB'S PAIN AND
GOD'S BLESSING

Laurie

I met my dear friend Laurie shortly after I moved to Florida. Laurie lived in our community which I affectionately called the compound, because we literally never had to leave the subdivision. All necessities were in the four walls, including food, friends, and fellowship.

Laurie and I met at our neighborhood Bible study. We became fast friends because we were like-minded lovers of Jesus who were all about His kingdom and His will in our subdivision. We would text in the wee hours of the morning because, well, she was up and I was up. We would text about the beautiful sunset the evening before or the spectacular morning moon. We would take long walks around our four-mile walled subdivision, sharing our life stories or solving the world's problems as we women often do. We'd pray for God to help all involved.

At the time, Laurie's husband was battling liver cancer, and he wasn't doing well.

It was a long process of doctor visits and experimental treatments. Laurie took him all over Southwest Florida for special therapies and medicines.

Laurie is a fighter and a warrior for her husband, especially when it comes to the things of God. Laurie believes our heavenly Father is a God of miracles, and she has a way with complete strangers and insists on pointing them to Jesus. She likes to say, "He's the way of our hope," and loves hosting those who are downtrodden. She has a special and unique way of loving them—from the cashier at Kroger, to the maintenance man in her garage, to the CEO of her insurance company, to the storm shutter company owner.

As her husband's health continued to decline, Laurie was insistent she would keep him home with her right through death. We all knew it would be a difficult passing, as I imagine most deaths are.

I asked her, "Laurie, are you sure you don't want to take him to the hospice?"

An always kind, but emphatic "No" would be her reply.

The inevitable happened one endless evening. We wept and reminisced together.

Bob's large, extended family was coming to Florida for the funeral. There was much to prepare. *Where would everyone sleep? What meals would she make?*

Laurie's thoughts swirled with these questions. They were coming down for her and for her boys. They were coming to mourn their dear brother. She understood. The burden of Bob's passing was great for everyone who loved him. She put her head down and went to work. She made Martha Stewart look like an intern.

Laurie's many extraordinary talents for hospitality exude from her.

Besides being a master chef, her gift-wrapping is nothing short of Bloomingdale's quality. She can decorate a room, a table, or a plate as if the President was coming. She's amazing and everyone knows it.

I've been the recipient of her beautiful presentations on more than one occasion. I never want to open her gifts or dig into her meals because I'm so often awestruck by the beauty of them.

During the time of Bob's extended family visiting, Laurie was definitely in her sweet spot. She was the hostess with the mostest. I could see this business helped her in her grief.

When all her possible responsibilities were over and she was ready, we would resume our walks.

Laurie has two sons, ages twenty-eight and thirty-two.

Her older son came home from law school to take care of Laurie as well as grieve Bob. Her younger son, Matt, already lived at home because he suffered from physical ailments and was often bedridden.

One morning about eight months after Bob had passed, Laurie and I were taking our usual morning stroll around the community. That day we spent much of our time sharing about heaven. We talked about what we knew about it from the scriptures and we shared our wild imaginations about what we thought it would be like.

Laurie shared, "I know Bob. He's bending Jesus' ear. You know he's an attorney and always has deep, penetrating questions. I can hear him now … 'Jesus, how did you get those gigantic dinosaurs in the ark? Did it smell after so many months?' Bob loved details."

She was sure he was golfing. Before he passed, Bob hadn't been able to golf for many months.

What joy was on her face knowing how happy Bob was! His suffering had been great in the end. Yet, thinking of Bob in heaven brought some lightheartedness to Laurie, as well as a little reprieve. She shared with me about Bob's funeral that was held in the northeast with his extended family and how she got up and spoke that day.

"By God's power only," she said.

We had a delightful conversation, and as we were rounding the bend back home, I asked her about the rest of her day.

"I have a busy day of errands to catch up on." So we left, both feeling encouraged.

Early that evening, around 5:00, I received a call from a friend in the community. Her name is Julie. She knew that Laurie and I were friends.

"Cindy, have you talked with Laurie? Is she okay?"

"Yes, I left her around 9 this morning. Why?"

"I drove by her house and there's emergency vehicles and yellow tape around her house."

"What?"

I jumped in my car and drove the two miles around the lake to her home.

As I pulled up, I saw no emergency vehicles, no vehicles at all, no yellow tape. *What is Julie talking about?* I thought.

Laurie's front entry door is a massive double door with glass and iron. It's stunningly beautiful. Bob spared no expense when it came to his bride. They loved each other so much. They had thirty years of love.

I could see Laurie inside on the phone. I went to the door. Laurie noticed me through the glass and opened her door.

She blurted, "Chad is dead!" Her oldest son had died. Shocked out of my mind, I grabbed her and we hugged and sobbed.

Later, we sat at her kitchen table with Matt, who had come from his room looking for something to eat. I hugged him and gave him condolences.

I mean, what do you say?

There were family pictures strewn over the kitchen table. We sat together, looking at them while Matt ate.

Job and Laurie

What happened that day?

Laurie came home from running her errands and noticed Chad was not up. It was 12:30 pm., so it was unlike him. So she went back to check on him. When he didn't answer the door, she popped her head in and found him lying dead in his bed, completely blue and stiff.

We remembered our conversation from that morning and how we had talked about heaven. Now, Laurie had both her husband and her son in heaven in the same year, both of them way too young for death. One thing she declared that day was that she was confident, deep in her bones, that God had taken her son home to heaven. God had decided it was time for his death. Laurie had studied the God of the scriptures and knew Him well. She knew Him too well to deny this truth.

In the book of Job, Job would say the same thing. He always knew God was master over his life.

Laurie's young son's untimely death was too sudden for her, yet there was supreme comfort in knowing God had the best plan for Chad.

Isaiah 57:1-2 (NLT) states this sentiment. "Good people pass away; the godly often die before their time. But no one seems to care or wonder why. No one seems to understand that God is protecting them from the evil to come. For those who follow godly paths will rest in peace when they die."

Laurie knew that was true for Chad.

The months ahead were grueling. We talked, walked, and cried. Laurie went into hibernation for a while. I didn't blame her for doing so.

Many would describe Laurie as a person with great faith. They'd say she was so strong and had amazing strength with unwavering conviction. But she would tell them that it was all God holding her up.

One thing Laurie never did was curse the God Who took her son away from her.

Job never cursed God either, even though his wife encouraged him to.

Laurie also sought Jesus in her grief and she'd say that God supplied all of her needs in her mourning.

She would often get alone with God. If she was busy with obligations, she'd remind herself it was time to get alone with Jesus, especially when she was out of sorts.

He was the One Who brought all her strength so she could move. She didn't seek to understand why God did this but she trusted He knew what was best.

There is something to be said about a person who knows Jesus this well.

Laurie is a strong warrior who clings to Jesus' hope, help, strength, and comfort. Her satisfaction comes from Jesus.

God's Activity in the Book of Job: A Shocking Revelation

In Job 1:12 (NIV), God gave Satan permission to destroy Job, *"Very well, then, everything he has is in your power, but on the man himself do not lay a finger."*

We can learn much about Satan's control over humanity and his abilities to affect us from observing these few words. We can also learn much about God's ultimate authority and His granting permission over the governing of people's lives.

Earlier in the passage, we read that Job had been blessed by God. The work of his hands, his flocks, and his household were all entirely fruitful, abundant, and extravagant.

How did he gain this superb life? God gave it to him.

We also find out that Job lived a God-honoring life. God described Job's character as pleasing, blameless, and upright.

Wow. Wouldn't you love to have the Lord God Almighty describe your life in such holy language? Job was called *"a man who fears God and shuns evil"* (Job 1:8b [NIV]).

Now you might be prone to think that a man so good, upright, and blameless would be in God's perfect protection and favor, right? Aren't there many scriptures that seem to say if we walk blamelessly, we get preferential treatment?

Psalm 1:1-3 (NIV) tells us, *"Blessed is the man ... whose delight is in the law of the Lord; ... [he] is like a tree planted by streams of water, which yields its fruit in season and whose leaf does not wither—whatever they do prospers."*

Well, this was not so for Job. We will see that even his friends believed if a person was righteous, he would be favored and all would go well for them.

Job's downfall began when Satan, under the Lord's permission, put the sword to Job's servants, oxen, and donkeys. Even the "fire of God fell from heaven and burned up the sheep and the servants." This escalated to the death of his sons and his daughters (Job 1:16b [NIV]).

God gave Satan permission to kill Job's family; only his wife was spared. Job's response to this was worship: *"He fell to the ground in worship and said: 'Naked I came from my mother's womb and naked I will depart. The Lord gave and the Lord has taken away; may the name of the Lord be praised"* (Job 1:20-1 [NIV]).

Now those would not be the words on my tongue. If my family was killed and if everything I loved was taken away from me, I'd look at Job's words and say, "What? That's crazy language. That is a ridiculous attitude to have from such a tragic event."

I remember a friend of ours once said something I still remember to this day. After he got news that his high-school-age son had broken his neck and severed his spine during a basketball game, his response was, "God is good all the time."

When another friend of ours lost his young wife to breast cancer, he walked to the white board in her hospice room and wrote "God is good all the time."

I was there to witness him write the words.

Tell me, how can people proclaim such truths during such tragic events? Instead of waiting for a feeling of understanding to come while in the midst of devastating circumstances, my friends worshiped God as Job did.

These people knew a truth that was as solid to them as stone and was as firm to them as a foundation of titanium. That truth was this. God had done this thing, He was good, and He knew best. They believed this and acted on it.

1 Thess. 5:18 (NIV) says, *"Give thanks in all circumstances; for this is God's will for you in Christ Jesus."*

Job understood this. He knew Who had done this to his family. It wasn't Satan, it was God allowing Satan to move. He knew Satan was just a speck of dust in the eyes of his Almighty God. Any power

Satan had was because God gave it to him for His (sovereign) purposes. That's what Job intimately knew.

He described this in his words quoted above which are essentially, "Naked I came, naked I'll leave. I had nothing to do with this horrifying situation nor did anybody else. It was God Himself."

Interestingly, the next verse after this event says, *"In all this, Job did not sin against God by charging God with wrongdoing"* (Job 1:22 [NIV]).

Why? Because Job believed God knew what He was doing.

God is always 100 percent right. He is completely good to us. He's all-loving. If His fatherly hand causes something to happen, it's for the best.

Justified Pity

The Lord talked with Satan and reminded him of Job's blameless character even after his recent tragic loss of servants, livestock, and all of his sons and daughters. The Lord said to Satan, *"he still maintains his integrity, though you incited me against him to ruin him without any reason"* (Job 2:3b [NIV]).

Satan continued to taunt the Lord and said in essence, "Job will curse you if you harm his physical being." Although God granted Satan permission to harm Job physically, He didn't allow him to take his life. Under God's arrangement, Satan brought painful sores all over Job's body. At this point even his wife said, *"Curse God and die!"* (Job 2:9b [NIV]).

Job's response was, *"'You are talking like a foolish woman. Shall we accept good from God, and not trouble?' In all this, Job did not sin in what he said"* (Job 2:10 [NIV]).

Job kept truth right in front of his face all the time.

What truth? The truth that God was in control of his misery.

Although Satan was given permission to harm Job, God had a plan, and Job was sure it was a good plan. That is why Job's response was to worship God after he heard bad news.

Back in Job 1:21 (NIV), when Job heard that all he owned was destroyed and all his family was killed, he preached this truth to himself, *"The Lord gave and the Lord has taken away; may the name of the Lord be praised."* This wasn't his wishful thinking. Job had an absolute certainty in God's character.

I want to be that certain of God and His ways, don't you?

Because he preached this truth, Job spared himself from falling into the sin that I call "justified pity." Now there is no such thing as this type of pity. That's right. Why? Because of God's sovereignty in every single molecule of existence.

If I were Job, I think I'd say, "God isn't good or righteous. He isn't in ultimate control and He certainly doesn't love me."

Yet if God has done it, how can we feel self-pity?

His doings are always supremely good. I referred to justified pity earlier only because we can really sympathize with Job's misery. However, many people fall into unjustified self-pity.

Really, it is just not being able to see God's goodness while we are in suffering. So, like Job, we must put God and what we know about His love for us at the center of our lives. We must trust Him even when we do not feel or see a molecule of His goodness yet.

From Charles Spurgeon's sermon on God's providence based on Ezekiel 1:15-19 he says,

"I believe that every particle of dust that dances in the sunbeam does not move an atom more or less than God wishes ... the fall of ... leaves from a poplar is as fully ordained as the tumbling of an avalanche."[24]

When I Cried

Three of Job's friends showed up and tried to comfort him. No one said a word for seven days. The silence was broken by Job cursing the day of his birth.

This is in chapter 3 of Job.

I admit I cried like an erupting volcano when I read this chapter. I'm not a crier like John, my husband. He cries at Hallmark movies, and I laugh at him.

Why did I cry?

Because I entered into what Job must have been feeling. Everything was so incredibly hard. There was so much physical and emotional pain. Yet nobody seemed to care—not his wife and not even God—when He looked at his affliction. God was seemingly nowhere to be found. Job said, "*I have no peace, no quietness; I have no rest, but only turmoil*" (Job 3:26 [NIV]).

"*Why is life given to a man whose way is hidden, whom God has hedged in?*" (Job 3:23 [NIV]).

"Whom God hath put, as it were, in a prison, so that he can see no way or possibility of escape; but all refuge fails him."[25]

I cannot say in reality that God didn't care. Yet because of my lack of understanding of God's purpose for the future and for the things of God, and because of my ignorance, it seems like He didn't care.

Indeed, there can be no truth in my statement because God does know and does care for us more than any person on earth. His love for His chosen servants is well off the charts.

So often we must stand on what is true. This is why I wrote this book. So we can see that even in the hard, hard, hard, God is with us, securing His good purpose.

Friends of Job

In Job 5, Job's friends began to question his character.

These friends had such good counsel to give Job. "*You have supported those who stumbled; you have strengthened faltering knees. But now trouble comes upon you and you are discouraged ... should not your piety be your confidence and your blameless ways, your hope?*" (Job 4:6 [NIV]).

Think about this, Job, "*Who, being innocent, has ever perished? Where were the upright ever destroyed?*"

Job, "*those who plow evil and those who sow trouble reap it. At the breath of God, they perish; at the blast of his anger they are no more*" (Job 4:7-9 [NIV]).

Would we follow the same line of questioning to our friends if they were Job? "Do right, Job, come on, confess your sins so you can have a blessed life again."

Job's friends thought this. If I'm honest, I've sometimes thought the same thing. Too often I can be judgmental about a situation.

These men pleaded with Job, as I know I would have done with my dear friend ... *"if I were you, I would appeal to a God; I would lay my cause before him"* (Job 5:8 [NIV]).

Couldn't you see yourself pleading to your friend, "Cry out to the One who can help you and deliver you."

They went on.

"He performs wonders that cannot be fathomed, miracles that cannot be counted" (Job 5:9 [NIV]).

"He provides rain for the earth, he sends water on the countryside ... those who mourn are lifted to safety" (Job 5:10 [NIV]).

"Blessed is the one whom God corrects; so do not despise the discipline of the almighty. For he wounds; but he also binds up; he injures, but his hands also heal. We have examined this, and it is true. So hear it and apply it to yourself" (Job 5:17-18, 27 [NIV]).

The men continued.

Now, please tell me, wouldn't you say exactly the same words of desperation to your friend in their torment?

Job's friends talked about how compassionate God was. How He was the only One who could deliver the help that Job needed. God brought rain to the earth. He performed miracles and wonders. He was able to care for Job's wounds.

"Come on, Job, please."

From the perspective of Job's friends, it seemed like Job might have done something wrong.

The friends did not see God's purpose and they made assumptions based on their limited knowledge of God.

This was a Proverbs 18:17 (NIV) case. *"The first to speak seems right, until someone comes forward and cross examines."*

There's a couple of very important things to look at in this story. God had said Job was completely blameless, righteous, and upright; He said Job was someone who shunned evil and feared God. Yet Job's friends thoroughly vetted their assessment and believed that their appraisal was plainly right. They said, "We examined this thinking." Yet we find Job's friends' assessment was wrong even though it seemed so accurate to them. The friends' assessment: "We examined this thinking. We thoroughly vetted it. Our appraisal is plainly right."

BUT God.

What are we learning with Job's friends and Job's character?

God's ways are not our ways, they are higher and heavenly (Isaiah 55:8-11 [NIV]).

This is God's upside down kingdom.

Isaiah 29:16 (NIV) says, *"You turn things upside down as if the potter were thought to be like the clay! Shall what is formed say to the one who formed it, 'You did not make me'? Can the pot say to the potter, 'You know nothing?'"*

We are but pots in the hands of our Great Potter.

A Godly Perspective

Facts demand our minds and hearts to center on God. Not on our interpretation of what we think He's doing.

How often do we reason out (with our incomplete minds) "This must be what's going on." Much like Eve did in the garden with the serpent, she reasoned out a completely false narrative. She thought if she ate the forbidden fruit it would give her wisdom to be like God, which was something she thought she wanted but did not have yet.

She believed God hadn't given her everything. She believed she was missing out on something, specifically wisdom.

It's a dangerous thing to think God is withholding something from you. It is wrong thinking.

We are called to put Him in the center of every event in our life.

As Charles Spurgeon said in his sermon on Ezekiel, "Every single speck of dust on your glass table is in his solidarity plan. Not an atom out of place. Oh, what freeing this gives our tangled hearts. What confidence to our hurting souls. What lightheartedness it brings to our thoughts."[26]

What we can learn from Job's tragedy so far is to bow our heads in struggles and worship as he did. This means to acknowledge God in the struggle. This truth keeps our heads on straight in the doubt, sorrow, self-pity, guilt, resentment, fear, anger, and hopelessness that flood in on us. We must, with every last drop of gumption drummed up in our minds and hearts remember that God is good ALL the time, most exceptionally when we can't see it. Let's do this as runners running a race to get a prize.

Job's Replies

Job replied to his friends' propositions.

Chapter 6 began with how Job was feeling: "*If only my anguish could be weighed and all my misery be placed on scales! It would surely outweigh the sands of the seas ...*"

I used to tell our son, Adam, "I love you more than the sand on the seashore," meaning I couldn't even begin to explain how much I loved him. It was outside of any bounds I could word. That's what Job was saying here about his intense anguish.

Job said, "*The arrows of the Almighty are in me, my spirit drinks in their poison; God's terrors are marshaled against me*" (Job 6:4 [NIV]).

Wow! Those are strong and negative poetic lyrics. Who's torturing him? God, he says. Imagine what his friends were thinking. What would you do if your friend was suffering and being tortured, and then blamed God?

What is the truth? Let's examine and dissect what the scripture tells us. What was Job saying?

Job wished God would end his life. "*That God would be willing to crush me. To let loose his hand and cut off my life!*" Job claimed almighty God had done all this misery to him and that God had crushed his family, livestock, and even his own being.

As a younger person, I remember realizing that God was in

complete, intimate control over all my moments. I previously thought God could be only over good moments because, after all, He's good and no evil exists around Him. But I have learned from the scriptures that while He is all good, He is also over evil and allows it for His good purposes as these verses tell us in Isaiah 45:7 (NIV),

"I form the light and create darkness, I bring prosperity and create disaster; I, the Lord, do all these things."

Job knew something I'm just recently learning. Nothing happens without God's purpose in it. Job gave God credit for his misery because he knew the supremacy of God in all things.

As hard as it is to accept, there's a comfort in knowing this. The comfort comes in the hard. God has good reasons even when I can't understand any of them.

Could God have chosen Job because of his understanding of Him? I don't know.

I'm left with Isaiah 55:8-11 (NIV): *"For my thoughts are not your thoughts, neither are your ways my ways. 'As the heavens are higher than the earth, so are my ways higher than your ways and my thoughts than your thoughts.'"*

I don't quite understand what God was doing to Job, but what I do grasp is that He was God back then, He's God now, and He has a supreme purpose.

Imagine Job telling YOU this.

His reason for wanting God to put an end to his existence was so that he wouldn't deny his Lord.

"Wait just one unbelievable minute, Job. You say you're 100 percent sure God has done this horrific thing to you and your entire family, friends, livestock, and home, and your response is to end your life because you don't want to deny Him?"

Oh, the love and understanding Job had for God. I am undone by his devotion to his King of Kings and his deep comprehension. It's as if he had already been to heaven and had seen the purpose in all of his pain.

I have a friend with ALS. She's near the end now. There's suffering but there's also complete peace. Why? Because years ago, she had one of those near-death experiences and she now knows that the inexhaustible and wonderful next is coming to her!

What a kindness it is of the Lord to give that to her.

God's mercy in our affliction is extreme. It's very hard when you're the one looking at a situation from the outside. The person in the pain has the mercy of God, not you, the bystander.

When God called Abraham to sacrifice his son Isaac on the altar, it seems that God gave Abraham a dispensation, a faith he hasn't given me to do the unthinkable.

We know the end of the story. At the last second, God provided a ram for the sacrifice and Isaac was spared.

God takes us to the brink and builds up our faith all along the way. Keep the long view in your trials.

Purple Trees

What if you were Job's friend?

How would you counsel him at this point? What words of help would you give to him?

Would you be with his wife, as I would, when she said, "*Are you still maintaining your integrity? Curse God and die!*" (Job 2:9 [NIV]).

Even Job's wife understood that God Almighty had afflicted him.

Remember his friend's advice? "*Blessed is the one whom God corrects*" (Job 5:17 [NIV]).

They thought, *Job, you must have done something wrong. Appeal to God.*

From everything we know about our good God, his friend's argument seems logical. If we were Job's friends, our reasonable minds would probably deduct a similar answer to Job's scenario.

We are just like Job's friends, aren't we?

There is so much to learn from God's ways versus our human logic and how we deduct spiritual things.

Speaking of logic ... I took a logic class in college. Day one, the professor put all the class chairs in a big circle and he stood in the center of it. He proceeded to tell us there was a purple tree growing out of the floor. With logic, he taught us that given A plus B, we could reason C.

I got lost at the purple tree, thinking, "What am I doing in this class? I'm a science major, not an art major."

We have a lot of deductions and reasoning going on in our complex, God-given minds. But God lives outside of our reasonable thoughts. He expands our understanding of Him.

We will never completely grasp Him. What we are to do is trust Him and worship Him.

Proverbs 3:5-6 (NIV) tells us, *"Trust in the Lord with all of your heart."* Not your mind but your heart, your control center, *"and lean not on your own understanding."* Not your logical mind trying to reason it all out, but *"in all of your ways acknowledge him"* (put Him in the center of all of it whether you understand or not) *"and he will make your paths straight."*

In His planning throughout the Bible, God has never been A plus B equals C. This is evident through His upside-down ways.

He's F to B, maybe G, isn't He?

Faith and logic are not two sides of the same coin but faith and trust are. I want to allow God to enter my logical mind.

Wrestling with Tragedy

With this in mind, let's look at how Job answers his friends. *"What strength do I have, that I should still hope? What prospects, that I should be patient? ... do I have any power to help myself ..."* (Job 6:11, 13 [NIV]).

Job continues for many verses on this theme. He seemed to think, "Who can help me? no one." He then turned his attention to God and said, *"What is mankind that you make so much of them, that you give them so much attention, that you examine them every morning and test them every moment? Will you never look away from me or let me alone even for an instant?"* (Job 7 :17-19 [NIV]).

Job again put blame for his misery on where blame was due. God has done this, and He did not relent. Job could not understand why God did it to him. He could not fathom why his almighty God did this horrible thing to him. He couldn't see God's long view.

That's the thing we must wrestle with. God is God His way. His plans are His and He created us.

His love and His understanding no one can fathom. Darkness to us is full light to Him. One day when believers all get to Heaven, we will have these hard things answered and we will say then, "Yes, Lord, Your way was best."

He is the One who brought us to the tiny speck of planet earth in His expansive, 100 billion galaxies we know of today. He created you and me out of love for us. He chose us before He even created the world. In love, He chose us; He adopted us for His pleasure and will. Read it in Ephesians 1.

He then sent His ONLY Son, whom He loved, to die a horrible, tortured death for you and me so that we could be adopted into His family. He's now our Father Who art in heaven.

He holds all our pain in His capable, fatherly hands. Every tear we shed falls into His jars in Heaven.

Charles Spurgeon puts it this way: "the God of providence has limited the time, manner, intensity, ... and effects of all our sicknesses, each throb is decreed each sleepless hour predestined ... nothing escapes the ordaining hand of Him who numbers the hairs of our head.

"Affliction is not a haphazard event. He who made no mistakes in balancing the clouds ... commits no errors in measuring out the medicine of our souls.

"The knife of the heavenly surgeon never cuts deeper than necessary. He who fixed the bounds of our habitation has also fixed the bounds of our tribulation."[27]

Isaiah 45:9 says, *"Woe to those who quarrel with their Maker, those who are nothing but potsherds among the potsherds on the ground. Does* the clay say to the potter, 'What are you making?' Does your work say, 'The potter has no hands'?"

How to Comfort Grieving Friends

Job's friends doubled down. "You must have done something wrong" because *"Does God pervert justice? Does the Almighty pervert what is right? When your children sinned against him, he gave them over to the penalty of their sin. But if you will seek God earnestly and plead with the Almighty, if you will become pure and upright ... he will restore you back to your prosperous state"* (Job 8:3-6 [NIV]).

"Surely God does not reject one who is blameless or strengthen the hands of evildoers" (Job 8:20 [NIV]).

Job was chosen by God for Satan's supposed use because he was upright and blameless and would not curse God (Job 1:8). So as logical as the friend's appeal seemed, they did not understand or take into account the unknown plan of God.

Job understood the Who. It was God doing the deed. The unknown was the why.

The friends thought they understood why.

I have learned to be so very careful when I think I have God figured out. He's not a man that lives in our human understanding. There is no parameter that could ever hold Him. He's outside all our deductive or analytical reasoning.

My question is (and I'm sure your question is too), *Well then, what should we say or do when our friend is hurting?*

We have learned from Job and his friends that God is always involved. We must not presume the worst.

We must let the struggling person know that God has not left them.

We must let them know He is holding them with His fatherly hands even though, as in Job's case, not a bone in his body felt it. Our hurting friend may not feel it either. It doesn't mean God has left them. Just the opposite. Because of God's great love, He is working. It means God trusts them with a high calling of suffering for some good plan they cannot see.

What we need is truth with love to bring us the hope and help that God promises (Proverbs 3:5-6).

Job, in his greatest grief, grabbed hold of God.

We often feel afraid to say that God is involved in our grief.

In our humanness, this can be a hard reality for us to accept, but for Job, it was a tender, true, hopeful, and kind reality.

God's Mercies and Grace

In chapter 9, Job responded to his friends. "God's not rejecting those who are blameless ... *I know that this is true ...*" Job knew God's character was proof of that. *"But how can mere mortals prove their innocence before God?"* (Vs. 2). There was nothing he could do to make God change His mind or prove to Him that he was innocent. Job continued by God's power, knowing His ultimate strength was over every single molecule in the universe. *"He moves mountains without their knowing it ... He speaks to the sun and it does not shine ..."* I have no recourse. (Job 9:2, 5, 7 [NIV]).

Take a moment to think about the reality of God's controlling power over creation. Job understood it.

"How can I find words to argue with him?" (Job 9:14 [NIV]).

We see how weary Job is: *"If I summoned him and he responded, I do not believe he would give me a hearing. He would crush me with a storm and multiply my wounds for no reason"* (Job 9:16-17 [NIV]). Job was hopelessly devastated. Words like *crush me* and *multiply my wounds* show us how overcome he was by his disastrous situation. How can we read this story and blame Job?

I just heard a sad story about a young woman who miscarried her twins. She has an oldest son who is diagnosed with ADHD and OCD, and a youngest child who is autistic. To add on even more tragedy, her mom was killed in a car accident with her oldest son in the car. Her son now blames himself for the accident.

This seems like a Job story. How could you move forward in this tragically horrible situation?

BUT GOD. He will give this young mom everything she needs to finish well through her tragedy. It's the promise of our God, Who always has a purpose. When I heard her story my heart sank to the depths of despair for her. But then I quickly reminded myself of the truth. God has not left her, and He will give the grace (a gift) needed to triumphantly get through it. I've experienced this in my own life.

It's true for each of us.

There are treasures coming even in our storms.

Therefore, I have hope *"Because of the Lord's great love we are not consumed, for his compassions never fail. They are new every morning; great is your faithfulness."* (Lamentations 3:23-24 [NIV]).

Job reminded himself that God was in charge over all his misery.

"When a land falls into the hands of the wicked, he blindfolds its judges. If it is not he, then who is it?" (Job 9:24 [NIV]).

I'm undone by that verse because I cannot understand why either. I've not been given insight by God. So I bow my head in reverent submission, knowing God has His heavenly plans (Isaiah 55:8-11 [NIV]).

Running the Race

This lack of understanding, as Job experienced, can create an extremely painful road for someone like my friend's wayward daughter, Abby, who is a precious woman of God.

Why would she abandon her family and her young daughters at such a vulnerable age? Why would she completely abandon her faith and her husband for booze and a scandalous life?

It is not understandable, it is unbelievable. It's as if someone else took over her body and her mind. We are completely shattered like her family is. Her children and husband groan before the Lord. Reading this story of Job and God's interaction in his life has helped me see He does not leave His people unattended or uncared for. I just don't get to know His way. But I do know HIM who does not do things willy-nilly. His ways are divine, unimaginable to my finite mind. His plans, well, they are never thwarted (Job 42:2).

Yet the pain in this case is excruciating.

My friend and I cry out together for some comfort during this horrendous loss. I pray to be a good friend, not a Job-friend. There is no choice for us but to put God in the center of what's happening to this dear woman. That's the truth.

And we know this truth is what sets us free, as the apostle John said (John 8:32).

There's comfort here for my friend because His fatherly hands are all over this dear woman's life. God help her. I do not understand. That has to be enough, for now. HE performs wonders that cannot be fathomed and miracles that cannot be counted (Job 5:9). My friend and I keep this fact in the forefront of our disgusted, exhausted, bone-tired minds. This is the strain for the prize in the race God has us run on. We run as those who are running for a prize. We beat our body into submission as a marathon runner of the faith.

1 Corinthians 9:24-26 (NIV) tells us, *"Run in such a way as to get the prize. Everyone who competes in the games goes into strict training. They do it to get a crown that will not last, but we do it to get a crown that will last forever. Therefore I do not run like someone running aimlessly; I do not fight like a boxer beating the air."*

As God's people, we are running in full training. Life is at stake.

Could this be what God teaches us through Job's life?

I want to tighten my bootstraps and put on my marathon gear. God has called me to persevere in faith, so that's what I'm going to do, whatever it takes.

How about you? Do you need to get those battle boots on? Do you need to bring in foxhole friends to help hold you up? They're waiting for you, I'm sure. Call them today and ask for help, you child of the King. God wants to put in the battle soldiers who are ready to fight.

For Those Who Are Depressed

I believe that this next part Job shares is for all those who are weary, depressed, and taken over by life's struggles.

Listen to what he says. *"My days are swifter than a runner; they fly away without a glimpse of joy ... if I say, 'I will forget my complaint, I will change my expression, and smile,' I still dread all my sufferings"* (Job 9:25-28 [NIV]).

"I loathe my very life; ... Why then did you bring me out of the womb? I wish I died before any eye saw me" (Job 10:1, 18 [NIV]).

He uses more of this type of language. You get the picture.

Do you ever feel this worn out by your struggles? I have. I remember those times like it was yesterday. I bet you do too.

My first cancer thirty-eight years ago was exhausting and tragic. Chemo back then was not what it is today and the special drugs to ward off the side effects were still primitive.

I remember being in my bed, vomiting every single day and being threatened by my oncologist with dreaded hospitalization. I would lay curled up in pain, wishing it was over and wondering how I could ever do eight months of this torture. I thought for sure I would die. I begged God, "Where are You? Save me from this pit of hell I'm in." "Are you even listening, God?" "Do You even care, or are You not even able to help me?"

Day after day, this went on. There was so much back then that I didn't know about God. I learned from His word that it was He who had brought such excruciating struggle to me.

Why? Because through it, He was saving my eternal soul, showing His magnificent power and revealing His vast, personal, and fatherly care. These were lessons I could only see through such hard afflictions.

Job 36:15-16 (NIV) says, *"But those who suffer he delivers in their suffering, he speaks to them in their affliction. He is wooing you from the jaws of distress to a spacious place free from restriction, to the comfort of your table laden with choice food."*

I was learning in the struggle of my life to hold on to the tree of life, to God's fatherly hand. He was wooing me from the JAWS of distress to that beautiful, wonderful, spacious place, free from those gnarly, life-sucking restrictions. I had to hold on and listen to His voice. He was speaking, and I let Him talk His fatherly whispers to me.

He gives His adopted sons and daughters such tender comfort. The kind of comfort only He can give.

Listen to Job's grand finale after all his tragedy in Job 42:2-3 (NIV) (emphasis and notes mine).

Job replied to all God had done to him: *"I know that you can do all things; no purpose of yours can be thwarted."* (You see, he knew this fact all along.) *"You asked, 'Who is this that obscures my plans without knowledge?'"* (Take note: God reminds him of his total lack of understanding. That's us too.) *"Surely I spoke of things I did not understand, THINGS TOO WONDERFUL FOR ME TO KNOW."*

Remember all those verses in which he said it would have been better if he had never been born? He wanted death. He was so devastated in chapter 9 and 10. How did he go from wanting to end his life to: **"Things too wonderful for me to know"?**

Wow. Wow. Wow. I think we need to preach this to ourselves moment by moment in our suffering. Lord, help us do this.

Remind yourself in your suffering.

Keep your focus on the future, not the tragedy.

You can read all about my chemo struggle in *Tragedy Turned Upside Down.*

Job's Other Friend Zophar Enters the Picture

In chapter 11, we hear quite a stellar argument from Zophar, Job's friend. I find myself cheering him on as I read. Zophar says, *"Can you fathom the mysteries of God? Can you probe the limits of the Almighty? They are higher than the heavens above—what can you do? They are deeper than the depths below—what can you know? ... if he comes along and confines you to prison and convenes a court who can oppose him? Surely he recognizes deceivers; and when he sees evil does he not take* note? But the witless can no more become wise than a wild donkey's colt can be born human" (Job 11:7-12 [NIV]).

Was all of what Zophar said true? Yes. Yes it was.

In chapter 42:7b (NIV), God rebuked Job's three friends with hard words. *"I am angry with you and your two friends because you have not spoken the truth about me, as my servant Job has."*

The untrue words: "Job, you have sinned, otherwise this would not be happening to you. Get yourself right with God and He will make things go well for you again."

Read with me Job 11:13-19 (NIV): *"Yet if you devote your heart to him and stretch out your hands to him, if you put away the sin that is in your hand and allow no evil to dwell in your tent, then, free of fault, you will lift up your face; you will stand firm and without fear. You will surely forget your trouble, recalling it only as waters gone by. Life will be brighter than noonday, and darkness will become like morning. You will be secure, because there is hope; you will look about you and take your rest in safety. You will lie down, with no one to make you afraid, and many will court your favor."*

The three friends' views of hope: "If you will do right and put away your sin and keep evil from your home, then you will not have any more fear. All your troubles will be forgotten. Your life will be brighter than in the middle of the day. All your misery and darkness will leave you. You will be secure, and no one will make you afraid, and you will have God's favor."

The problem these three men very logically analyzed was 100 percent false.

God's penance for them is as follows in Job 42:8: *"So now take seven bulls and seven rams and go to my servant Job and sacrifice a burnt offering for yourselves. My servant Job will pray for you, and I will accept his prayer and NOT deal with you according to your folly."*

Reflections on Job's Friends

I would like to ask you another question about the story of my friend's wayward daughter, Abby. Now that you understand God's ways a little better from these passages in Job, if you were Abby's friend, would you tell her to confess her sin and do what's right so God would have favor? So that her life would be brighter than noonday and so she would have joy in the morning?

Or would you sit in dust mourning with her over her waywardness? Would you ask her, "How I can help you heal from what has taken over your beautiful faith?"

I don't know myself. I am caught between the two. While I want to scold her into submission to God, I know how God rebuked Job's friends for doing that. Perhaps it would be better to sit with her and weep for her pain.

So I pray, "Lord, teach me your ways to truly help my friends."

Job was on his last straw in Job 13:4-5 (NIV): "You ... smear me with lies; you are worthless physicians, all of you! If only you would be altogether silent! For you, that would be wisdom." In Job 16:2 he continued, "...you are miserable comforters, all of you!"

Ouch.

And in Job 19:2-3 (NIV): "How long will you torment me and crush me with words? Ten times now, you have reproached me; shamelessly, you attack me."

Again, ouch!

And in Job 19:21-22 (NIV): "Have pity on me, my friends, have pity, for the hand of God has struck me. Why do you pursue me as God does? Will you never get enough of my flesh?"

This language of Job is something to sit on and seriously consider before giving godly advice. The book of Proverbs tells us there are always two sides to every story, and we'd be fools not to listen to both sides (Proverbs 18:17 [NIV]).

Could that be a lesson for us? Hear out the person past the point of "I get it now, let me tell you what you should do."

Let yourself feel their side of the story as well as their pain. At all costs, put God in the center of what's going on. Ask for His wisdom for your friend, family member, or co-worker. As I read Job, I was gripped by my friend's daughter's pain. What could God be doing in all of this?

I'm reminded of the story of the prodigal son in scripture. The Lord brought this wayward son home from his rebellious lifestyle. The father patiently waited, and I'm sure he poured out prayers on behalf of his hell-bent child.

"There was a severe famine in that whole country, and he began to be in need ... When he came to his senses, he said, 'How many of my father's hired servants have food to spare, and here I am starving to death! I will set out and go back to my father and say to him: Father, I have sinned against heaven and against you. I am no longer worthy to be called your son; make me like one of your hired servants" (Luke 15:14, 17-19 [NIV]).

We don't know the son's motives except he was in need. But the father didn't care about his son's motives. He cared that his son returned. The father said, *"Quick! Bring the best robe and put it on him. Put a ring on his finger and sandals on his feet. Bring the fattened calf and kill it. Let's have a feast and celebrate!"* (Luke 15:23-24 [NIV]).

God provided the circumstances to bring that hell-bent son home. The father in the parable taught me the lavish love, grace, and mercy of God. I would have expected bitterness, anger, and vengefulness and for him to show his son a lesson or two.

Oh Lord, may I learn to give tenderness like the father in this parable.

Patient in Affliction

In chapters 12-14, with much emotion and graphic detail, Job laid out his agony and his wretchedness. He felt that God's angry hand was on him. It's frankly hard to read.

Job 13:24-27 (NIV): *"Why do you hide your face and consider me your enemy? Will you torment a windblown leaf? Will you chase after dry chaff? For you write down bitter things against me and make me reap the sins of my youth. You fasten my feet in shackles; you keep close watch on all my paths by putting marks on the soles of my feet."* God shows us His plans are not our plans. We must learn to be patient with affliction and remind ourselves that God is all good.

AW Tozer explains it like this: He's "kind, cordial, benevolent, full of goodwill toward men. He is tenderhearted and quick of sympathy, and His unfailing attitude toward all moral beings is open, frank, and friendly. By His nature He is inclined to bestow blessedness and he takes holy pleasure in the happiness of his people ... The goodness of God is the drive behind all the blessings He daily bestows upon us."[28]

These factual statements are a must when we are in affliction. Job had good days and bad days. Don't we, as well? If I was Job, I'd cry out, "God, bring real friends who will hold my arms up as Aaron did for Moses. Friends who will carry me through this nightmare. Keep those who will heap more misery on my head far from my tent."

One important note to take from chapter 14 is that Job put the blame on God for his sufferings, using lyrical language, "*As a mountain erodes and crumbles and as a rock is moved from its place, as water wears away stones and torrents wash away the soil, so you destroy a person's hope*" (Job 14:18-19 [NIV]).

Whew! Those are some excruciatingly painful words. This must be what a person acts like when hope is stripped away from them.

A note to myself; when I hear someone speak in contemporary language similar in theme and intensity to Job, I must remember that this person is seriously suffering. For them, hope has vanished.

Metaphorically speaking, I must sit next to that person with ashes over my head. I must sympathize with them. Then, at the right moment, I will have the favor to speak to that person because I listened before speaking.

What favor? The favor to speak life and truth right into their bare-naked hearts.

How can we know what to say? Well, we won't at first. But God will give us words at the right moment. We will be able to receive and deliver His words because our hearts will be open and pure, with no moral judgement.

Matthew 10:19 (NIV) says, *"But when they arrest you, do not worry about what to say or how to say it. At that time you will be given what to say."*

If in your situation you wish someone else could be there for a hurting person in your life because you believe he or she would be better at knowing exactly what to say, remind yourself that God has placed you in the situation, not someone you think is more qualified. At the moment, you're the most qualified. You're the one God picked for the task. So step it up, be lion-like, walk straight into that position, and let God breathe life into that hurting person through using you.

How to Comfort Others

I remember a time when our landscaper suddenly ended up in the hospital with a life-threatening brain tumor. It was shocking news to receive because he was such a young, athletic, healthy-looking, and hard-working guy.

I knew I needed to get to that hospital and talk with him.

God doesn't place such grave circumstances in front of us for us to lie down and shrink. No. When we feel like doing that, that's when it is exactly time to engage.

There were so many obstacles to overcome in this situation. Fear first. I asked myself if I should I go to the hospital alone. This young man really didn't know us at all. It was sudden news.

I thought to myself how hard it must have been for him to find out he had a brain tumor when he was only in his late 20s. Then thoughts came to my mind like, *He probably won't want to make conversation with his landscape customers.* But because I felt God was saying this was a serious situation, I pushed past my thoughts.

I reasoned to myself, *Who cares what any single person thinks? A man's life is hanging on by a thread.*

That thought was truly my motivation. I called John at work and told him about the situation. He agreed that the two of us should meet this man at the hospital even though neither of us had an inkling of what we were going to say to him.

"What room is Brian Helm in, please? Room 4041? "

John and I got in the elevator with three other people. We stopped on the second floor and then again on the third, which felt like the longest elevator ride of our life. We got to the fourth floor, and the door opened.

Neither of us wanted to step off. We hesitantly walked onto the fourth floor hallway where it was eerily quiet. It was luxuriously carpeted for a hospital with blue, gray, and brown tweed. It had a warm feel. A nurse passed by and asked if we needed any help.

John said we were looking for Brian Helms's room. She pointed to the room right in front of us.

"Honey, the door is closed," I said.

The nurse mentioned that Brian was down the hall and that he was meeting with his doctors.

Oh no, they are telling him his options.

This was the worst time in the world for us to be there.

"The door is closed," the nurse said. "The family is in the room."

What? *We can't go into that room. They're waiting for the bad news. How do we walk in and say "Hi, we are Brian's landscape customers." Seriously, God, now You have us here?*

I turned to John. "Guess we should leave. Let's go."

John said, "No, we came all the way. Let's just go in, introduce ourselves as Brian's clients, and tell them we have been here in our lives and we want to be an encouragement."

My thoughts raced. *How did I get here? It's my big mouth again, always jumping in to HELP. I could be home watching the evening news in my jammies right now and escape all this tragic pain.*

Yet all I could think of was, *Lord, please use us to comfort them.* We were scared to death, but we were also persistently passionate about helping this family.

I'm sure Job's friends felt the same way.

"Okay honey, you go in first " John opened the door to a room full of people. Fifteen people were crowded in that hospital room. They all looked at us with expression that said, "Who are you?"

Remember, they were waiting for Brian to return from talking to the doctor about his brain tumor options. Did I tell you he had a fiancé, Julie?

John introduced us just as he had rehearsed. What happened next was unbelievable. Everyone said, "Oh, you two talk with Brian. We will wait outside in the waiting room."

What? The landscaper clients had priority in hearing what the doctors were going to tell Brian and Julie? Crazy! But God was the One orchestrating our talk.

2 Corinthians 1:3-4 says, *"Praise be to the God and Father of our Lord Jesus Christ, the Father of compassion and the God of all comfort, who comforts us in all our troubles so that we can comfort those in any trouble with the comfort we ourselves receive from God."*

That's what we were about to do—comfort with the comfort we received. It wasn't going to be based on our wise words but on God's faithful breath through His obviously chosen servants.

When everyone left the room, it was just John and me left. We were shaking in our boots as we waited for them, still shocked by what God was orchestrating. We waited maybe ten minutes, which felt like five hours.

The door opened, and Brian walked in, surprised to see us instead of his family. Just like a choreographed dance, God took over and beautifully directed our conversation. John and I were able to bring great help, hope, and even Jesus to this young man who was about to be in the fight of his life.

Today, I'm forever grateful that John and I said yes to God. Despite all our fears and inadequacies, God used us to help that young couple and their family.

Questioning God

As we circle back to Job, let's look at chapters 15-16.

After Eliphaz (Job's friend) spoke, Job replied to him, *"Will your long-winded speeches never end? What ails you that you keep on arguing? I also could speak like you, if you were in my place; I could make fine speeches against you and shake my head at you. But my mouth would encourage you; comfort from my lips would bring you relief"* (Job 16:3-5 [NIV]).

If only Job could have had just one friend who understood, who showed compassion toward him, empathized with him, and helped soothe his scathing, raw, open sores.

How often is it that nothing relieves our pain? *"If I speak, my pain is not relieved. If I refrain, it does not go away!"* (Job 16:6 [NIV]).

Job explained before, *"All was well with me, but he shattered me, he seized me by the neck and crushed me. He has made me his target ..."* (Vs. 12). In many verses, Job declared that God caused his misery. *"Even now my witness is in heaven; my advocate is on high. My intercessor is my friend"* (Job 16:19-20a [NIV]).

He acknowledged God Most High.

Job desperately searched for a glimmer of light, a ray of hope. Bildad, his third friend, weighed in on Job's latest rant. *"When will you end these speeches? Be sensible, and then we can talk"* (Job 18:2 [NIV]). *"Surely you must be an evil man who does not know God"* (verse 21, my paraphrase.)

Can you imagine looking from the outside in on Job's story? Although we have confirmation that Job didn't sin, back then his friends firmly believed he had and they refused to believe otherwise.

It's easy to sympathize with Job's friends.

It's outlandish to think that our good God, our loving Father, would do this to His righteous, highly favored servant. Afterall, Job was a man who had not sinned. A pure man devoted to God.

Think about what God the Father did to his Son, Jesus. He hung Him on that horrible, tormentful cross.

How absurd is that?

From Don Steward in an article on Blueletterbible.org:

"The death of Christ was in the predetermined program of God

- planned before the foundation of the world. It is a crucial element in God's eternal plan to save humanity from their sins."[29]

God has a plan. His purpose is in all things.

Just as Jesus' death was His preplanned purpose. *"Indeed Herod and Pontius Pilate met together with the Gentiles and the people of Israel in this city to conspire against your holy servant Jesus, whom you anointed. They did what your power and will had decided beforehand should happen"* (Acts 4:27-28 [NIV]). We are forced to conclude that it is impossible to have a clear lens on God's purposes on this side of heaven. Jesus understood that when He said, *"Father, if you are willing, take this cup from me; yet not my will, but yours be done"* (Luke 22:42 [NIV]).

Jesus understood this truth of God when He asked to not suffer such excruciating pain.

2 Tim.1:12 (AMP) says, *"This is why I suffer as I do. Still, I am not ashamed; for I know Him [and I am personally acquainted with Him] whom I have believed [with absolute trust and confidence in Him and in the truth of His deity], and I am persuaded [beyond any doubt] that He is able to guard that which I have entrusted to Him until that day [when I stand before Him]."*

God's Perfect Character

When we are confronted with upside-down moments from God, we must remind ourselves of His perfect character, which is all loving, all good, all just, and all righteous. Even though it is not understandable to our finite minds, all His character traits coexist together. We must bow our heads in faithful trust to our faithful God. Or, said another way,

"Does the clay say to the potter, 'What are you making?'" (Isaiah 45:9b [NIV]).

Romans 9:20-21 (NIV) says, "But who are you, O man, a human being to talk back to God? Shall what is formed say to the one who formed it, 'Why did you make me like this?'"

We have no right to question God's plans or His motives.

Honor and Loyalty in Suffering

Job tried yet again to defend himself to his friends in Job 19. *"Know that God has put me in the wrong and closed his net around me ... He has walled up my way, so that I cannot pass, and he has set darkness on my paths"* (Vs. 6, 8.). *"My relatives have failed me, my close friends have forgotten me. The guests in my house and my maidservants count me as a stranger; I have become a foreigner in their eyes"* (Vs. 14-15). *"Have mercy on me, O you my friends, for the hand of God has touched me! ... For I know that my Redeemer lives ... whom I shall see for myself"* (Job 19: 21, 25, 27, [NIV]).

Job spoke the truth to himself even though no one helped him. What truth, you may ask? Although God afflicted him, He was still his God and his Redeemer. When he died, he would be with Him.

Job glorified God despite his torment.

Do you know of anyone who has given honor and loyalty to God while in severe suffering?

I think of when our son was dying at just five days old. He was a beautiful, perfect boy, and I knew God had afflicted him. Even though I was young in my faith, God was revealing His plans to me. Oddly, it was a rock-hard type of comfort to know God was caring for him while he was dying. I knew he was going home with Jesus to live out his life with our heavenly Father. This brought me great encouragement in my river of tears.

Eliphaz came to Job from another angle. In Job 22:3 (NIV) he said, *"Is it any pleasure to the Almighty if you are in the right, or is it gain to him if you make your ways blameless?"*

We can be 100 percent sure that Job was righteous and blameless. God chose him because of these two character traits.

The facts are, the Almighty was so pleased with Job that He picked him out of all the people on earth at that time for this purpose. Job was God's most devoted, purest choice.

I'm undone about God's plan for Job. It's upside down, which is why his friends were so messed up in their thinking. Eliphaz in Job 22:21, 23 (NIV) gave a compelling but completely untrue appeal to Job: "Submit to God and be at peace with him; in this way, prosperity will come to you ... return to the Almighty and you will be restored."

Job begged repeatedly, but only received crickets!

"If I could just get an audience with God, I would be delivered and judged innocent, but I cannot find him anywhere. He has kept his presence from me. Yet he knows the way that I take and when he has tested me, I will come forth as gold. My feet have closely followed his steps; I have *kept to his way without turning aside. I have not departed from the commands of his lips. I have treasured the words of his mouth more than my daily bread*" (Job 23:3-4, 10-12 [NIV]).

Despite all the naysayers, Job adamantly maintained his innocence.

The Truth

In Job 27:5 (NIV), Job said, "*I will never admit you are right [and I'm in sin]; till I die, I will not deny my integrity.*"

Why was Job so bent on truthfulness? Why wouldn't he concede and be set free from the oppression?

Could it be that it was because of his closeness with God and his humility in submitting to His authority against his rights as a blameless man, that the Lord chose him specifically? Job would not compromise. He was fully devoted to his God.

This is a huge learning curve for me. Will I let go of my rights? Will I give up what's fair when God's plan hurts me in the moment?

Maybe your hurt is over a wayward husband or wife or over an affair that has crushed you and left you for dead. Maybe you're under persecution, you've been royally wronged, or you feel like everyone is against you. Like Job, you can see the lies. Yet, because Jesus is your commander and chief, you bow your head and wait for your Deliverer, your Savior to come and rescue you.

"*People listened to me expectantly, waiting in silence for my counsel*" (Job 29:21 [NIV]). Job said, "that's the kind of man I was known as. I sat as the people's chief, as a king among the troops, one who comforts mourners. Now they mock me." He continued in Job

30:10-11 (NIV), "They detest me and keep their distance; they do not hesitate to spit in my face. Now that God has unstrung my bow and afflicted me, they throw off restraint in my presence."

As painful as it was, Job put truth into his circumstances and did not waver into falsehood. This was where his hope lied. God would bring him home to Heaven no matter what he suffered on earth.

"Have I not wept for those in trouble? Has my soul not grieved for the poor? Yet ... when I looked for light, then came darkness," said Job. He tried to understand. Why, Lord? (Job 30:25, 26 [NIV]).

Job reminded God of his heart of love for the downtrodden but only darkness came his way.

If I were in Job's situation, I'd be thinking and obsessing over my oh-so-striking dilemma. God does not live in our homemade boxes. He is outside of any human understanding unless He decides to reveal a hidden treasure.

See what Isaiah 45:3-7 (NIV) says: "I will give you hidden treasures, riches stored in secret places, so that you may know that I am the LORD, the God of Israel, who summons you by name. For the sake of Jacob my servant, of Israel my chosen, I summon you by name and bestow on you a title of honor, though you do not acknowledge me. I am the LORD, and there is no other; apart from me there is no God. I will strengthen you, though you have not acknowledged me, so that from the rising of the sun to the place of its setting, people may know there is none besides me. I am the LORD, and there is no other. I form the light and create darkness. I bring prosperity and create disaster; I, the LORD, do all these things."

There were no truer words than these for Job.

The Lord Enters

Job's friends said their defenses, and Job responded. In Job 38, God entered the scene.

God's first words to Job were, "Brace yourself like a man. I will question you and you shall answer me. Where were you when I laid the earth's foundation? Tell me, if you understand. Who marked off its dimensions? Surely you know! ... Who shut up the sea behind doors when it burst forth *from the womb? ... Have you ever given orders to the morning ... Do you know the laws of the heavens? Can you set up God's dominion over the earth? ... Do you watch when the doe bears her fawn?"* (Job 38:3-5, 8, 12, 33, 39:1b [NIV]).

This goes on for seventy-one verses.

God cut right into His supremacy.

I shrink to ant size as I read chapters 38-40. If you need a big dose of God's enormousness in your difficulty, sit down and read these chapters.

When I had just been diagnosed with breast cancer in both breasts and was waiting for a mastectomy, I needed God's enormous help in my sickness. Oh boy, did He show up. I cried to Him, "Lord, please talk with me and comfort me in this tragedy."

I opened my Bible to Job chapter 38 and began reading this list of questions God spoke to Job. Strangely, my fear dulled, and my contentment rose.

You might think, *Those are harsh words, Lord, for a suffering woman.*

But it was just the opposite. Comfort, confidence, strength, and encouragement began to fill what was my terrified and anxiously pounding heart. I felt greatly helped. My fear dissipated. Peace came over me like a warm blanket snuggling me on a cold night.

My God took take care of me. The following days were a blur, but God's enormousness never left me. His question, *"Where were you when I laid the earth's foundation?"* (Job 38:4, [NIV]), flooded my fretful mind and pushed all my fears to the sidelines.

What actions could I take to control my cancer situation, anyway? Not only did God take care of me, but He brought me treasures that were unimaginable gifts right in the middle of it all. A favorite gift I received was from our 16-year-old son who gave me a huge hug when he heard of my cancer news. He told me it was all going to be okay. That warm embrace from his 6-foot frame and God-confidence that he exuded at such a young age had to have been from the Lord. I knew then I was going to be alright.

As mentioned before, you can read more of this story in my book *Tragedy Turned Upside Down*.

As we circle back to God's rebuke of Job, the Lord said, *"will the one who contends with the Almighty correct him?"* (Job 40:2 [NIV]). Job responded, *"I am unworthy"* (Job 40:4a [NIV]). What else could he say?

The crowning jewel of this incredible book of Job is chapter 42.

All the answers we have been wondering about lie in this chapter.

Job responded to God in Job 42:2-3 (NIV): *"I know that you can do all things;"* (Job reminded God of His endless abilities,) *"no purpose of yours can be thwarted. You asked, 'Who is this that obscures my plans without knowledge?' Surely I spoke of things I did not understand, things too wonderful for me to know."*

What? Things too what? What? What? Wonderful to know!

How can that be after all Job had been through? Even his wife once said to him, "curse God and die" (Job 2:9).

"You said, 'Listen now, and I will speak; I will question you, and you shall answer me'" (Job 42:4, NIV).

Where have we heard that before? In Job 38 and 40: *"My ears had heard of you but now my eyes have seen you"* (vs. 5). Job was saying, "I only knew You, God, in one sense, but now, I have an intimate and special revelation of You that is so wonderful. I couldn't see it at first. I couldn't comprehend that it was possible or that out of this endless horror I'd see You, God, and Your lavish love.

Impossible! Unbelievable! Astonishingly preposterous!

"Therefore I despise myself and repent in dust and ashes" (Vs. 6).

I've prayed a similar prayer. "I repent, Lord, for all the Why Questioning. The lack of trust when You had my back. The wavering. The times I wanted to die because of my fatalistic attitude. My lack of belief because I felt righteous and thought I didn't deserve this wrath."

These must be the things Job was so grieved about.

When God shines His light on a situation, we often succumb to saying we are sorry.

The truth comes out. Despite how adamantly we felt, and despite how certain we had been about circumstances, we find out as Job's friends did, just how off base we were and just how much we missed the mark. We become undone and feel shame about the absurd assumptions we made.

Ahhh. It's good to take moments like this and think about our absolutes. Maybe we believe with unwavering clarity that we are right in a situation. But because of Job's friends, we should take a warmer, softer second look.

I often remind myself, "Cindy, you do not have all the answers though you think you do and you feel sure in your heart." At the very least, we should put God in the center of our circumstances. "Give thanks in ALL circumstances; for this is God's will for you in Christ Jesus" (1 Thess. 5:18 [NIV], emphasis mine). This is a great reminder to pull out at a moment's notice.

I suffered with this plight recently during Covid. I was so absolutely sure of my convictions surrounding Covid but God showed me some very biased opinions I was carrying around. One new belief I had to adopt was that I don't have all the answers.

I spent much time apologizing to those near to me. It was a humbling experience, and it was so good for me.

Today, I have more compassion and empathy for those who think differently than I. I'm grateful for the teaching God gave me even though I felt like it was the difficult way of teaching me.

God's Response to Job's Friends

Now we get the very best part of what we have been waiting for. We get to find out all the answers to Job's tragedies.

First, we read God's responses to Job's friends who had essentially told him, "You are in sin. If you would stop sinning, God will bless you and all your misery will cease."

The Lord's response to Job's friends was, *"I am angry with you and your two friends, because you have not spoken the truth about me, as my servant Job has"* (Job 42:7 [NIV]).

The Lord dealt with their unbelief. *"Sacrifice a burnt offering for yourselves. My servant Job will pray for you and I will accept his prayer and not deal with you according to your folly"* (Job 42:8 [NIV]).

What, Lord? I thought. *Wow. Was I off base in my analysis of Job's friends?*

We find out from the Lord that the friends were 100 percent wrong in their judgment of Job. It was not his unrighteousness that caused his suffering. It was God's sovereign decree. Job spoke clearly about his plight. "You have not spoken the truth about me, as my servant Job has" (Job 42:8 [NIV]).

What we can learn from Job's friends and God's rebuke:

1. **We must pause** and think about our relationships. Are we speaking truthfully?

2. **We must put God in the center** and trust Him to care for others' lives.

3. **We must console** others how God wants us to.

Jude 1:23 (NIV), tells us we are to: *"save others by snatching them from the fire; to others show mercy, mixed with fear—hating even the clothing stained by corrupted flesh."*

We are to gently pull our wayward friends away from sin and show mercy to those suffering. At the same time, we need to be careful not to become contaminated by others' sin.

Sometimes we just don't want to give up the feelings of comfort we get from our sins.

Those are the ones who need snatching.

I know a woman who is contaminated by her own sin. Many have approached her about it. The heartache is she just can't see it. She'd tell you she's a poor victim and she'd say her husband is the problem.

Have you ever met a person like that? They look for someone to take on their plight. People will grab the bait and compassionately start to encourage and try to bring hope.

Soon they find a black hole.

As my friend says, this is "pitiful pearl syndrome," in which the supposed victim just wants your undivided attention and your pity.

What a sad state of affairs. All who know these people run far away from them because of the spiral of misery they cause. Such misery feels like burning on the skin (Jude 1:23).

Scripture tells us not to become contaminated by their sin. We are to hate even their stained clothes. This is a fair warning not to get sucked into the abyss of unhealthy moods. It is a most grievous sin against God to blame someone else for our unhappiness. When we do so, we are saying, "God, You don't know what You're doing. I know what's best for me."

Stay the mercy course but with the fear of God when interacting with these victims.

Charles Spurgeon, June 15, sums this up well: "The Christian should never think or speak lightly of unbelief. For a child of God to mistrust his love, his truth, his faithfulness, must be greatly displeasing to him. How can we ever grieve him by doubting his upholding grace? Christian! It is contrary to every promise of God's precious Word that thou shouldst ever be forgotten or left to perish."[30]

God is so faithful to us.

God Restores Job

After God addresses Job's friends, He restores Job's fortunes. He gives him twice as much as he had given Job before.

Job 42:10-11 (NIV) tells us, *"The Lord restored Job's fortunes and gave him twice as much as he had before. All his brothers and sisters and everyone who had known him before came and ate with him at his house. They comforted and consoled him over all the trouble the LORD had brought on him ..."*

The most important line in this book is that the Lord had brought this trouble on Job. Job knew this the whole time and mentioned it more times than we can count. Although Job's friends denied his belief, God rebuked them.

Just like Job's friends, we often can't imagine God bringing hurt on anyone, so we deny the truth that He does. We must take a moment to stop when we can't understand God and try again.

We must stop putting God in our boxes of finite discernment. God is all love, He is all just, and His ways are all perfect. These are facts. He wants all people to know Him as almighty. To know Him as supreme.

God is the only ultimate authority and the only One with ultimate wisdom. He has infinitely holy abilities so He cannot be understood. He demands the utmost in all things. *"As the heavens are higher than the earth, so are my ways higher than your ways"* (Isaiah 55:9, [NIV]). His plans are higher than our plans. His plans are heavenly. We are earthly.

As we think of God creating disaster and working evil for good, let us remember Job's words: *"I spoke of things I did not understand, things too wonderful for me to know"* (Job 42:3b [NIV]).

Although Job went through very hard and painful circumstances he did not understand, in the end, he could say, *"too wonderful for me to know"* (Job 42:3 [NIV]).

Only God can give this kind of perspective to suffering.

"The Lord blessed the latter part of Job's life more than the former part" (Job 42:12a [NIV]). This tips over my thinking of tragedy. How about you? May we bow with our hearts positioned to receive the greater good of God.

God during Covid

A close friend of mine, Sue, along with her husband, Fred, contracted Covid. Because Sue was high risk, she wanted to get vaccinated. However, Fred had been talking with a friend who was a doctor who treated vaccine side effects and he had persuaded Fred to not get vaccinated. Well, both Sue and Fred came down with Covid. Feeling they could shake this themselves because they were both physically fit and active, they hunkered down to ride it out.

The only problem was that Fred, the healthier of the two, got sicker and sicker.

Eventually Sue called the doctor, who said to take him to the ER ASAP. It had already been nine days of Fred feeling terrible. Once he arrived, the ER admitted him immediately.

Fred's oxygen was critically low. He spent ten days in the hospital on oxygen. He was given many of the available remedies at the time. It was a lonely, scary time for him. Fred was so unsure of his future at the time that he even secured his will while in that lonely Covid room. Fred's mind played fearful games.

Meanwhile, Sue hunkered down at home, all alone. Afterall, who would be with her?

When Fred was released ten days later, he had gone from being a super athlete to needing to shower with a chair. This strong, healthy man had become a mere shell of a man. Slowly his strength and stamina came back. Not anything we'd call normal, but the chair eventually left the shower.

He remained among the living.

Fred and Sue are both so grateful to be alive. I know many who are reading this have stories much graver than this one, and I never want to minimize the trauma so many have experienced.

This couple said God gave them something more precious than gold or silver gifts in their difficult season of suffering. God humbled them and showed them their complete arrogance in thinking that they could overcome the Covid beast because they were so healthy. They shared about the pridefulness that surrounded them in their physical health and how they used to think they had great health because of their stellar job taking care of themselves.

They now bow down to God and believe in what HE wants for them.

They experienced much love from hospital staff who laid down their lives for those, in this case, who were not vaccinated. They learned these staff workers had forsaken their friends, family, and children because of round-the-clock much-needed care of Covid-positive patients.

This is not political. This was their situation.

Fred and Sue would tell you it was God's will for them to get Covid. They would tell you it was better for them to be afflicted than for them not to be. They saw so many wonderful attributes of God demonstrated to them during their time of illness.

They would tell you they learned, like Job, that they spoke of things they did not understand and did not know. They would tell you that they repented of a know-it-all attitude.

Fred says Covid made him chill out and not be so intense about trivial matters.

Today, both Sue and Fred are chill about life and are more devoted than ever to others and the things of God.

"Before I was afflicted I went astray" (Psalm 119:67 [NIV]).

Chapter Six

A TAR BASKET FOR
STARVING NATIONS

As we explore the book of Exodus, we will see God's supreme authority over Moses' life and how He's supreme over our lives too. God's purpose in calling and choosing Moses was for him to lead His people, the Israelites, straight through the Red Sea into a land flowing with milk and honey.

Quite a famous passage of scripture involves the words "milk and honey". What we can learn is how God preplanned Moses' story and how He is preplanning our stories too.

Setting the Scene

Let's set the scene—Moses' birth.

Pharaoh, king of Egypt, hated God's chosen people, the Israelites. Therefore, when they became too numerous to handle, Pharaoh's orders were given to have every Hebrew baby boy thrown into the river.

Imagine Moses' mom's response to this. Imagine her saying, "My son is a fine-looking child. I must hide him from the killers of my people."

But as Moses got bigger, she could not hide him any longer and reasoned, "I will put him in a tar-laced basket and set him into the river in a quiet place among the reeds."

But Moses' sister stood in hiding to see what would happen to her baby brother. Meanwhile, the pharaoh's daughter went down to the river to bathe. She noticed the basket, opened it, saw Moses crying, and felt sorry for him.

"'This is one of the Hebrew babies,' she said. Then his sister asked Pharaoh's daughter,

"'Shall I go and get one of the Hebrew women to nurse the baby for you?' 'Yes, go,' she answered. So the girl went and got [Moses'] mother" (Exodus 2:6-8 [NIV]).

Pharaoh's daughter said to Moses' mom, "Take this baby and nurse him for me, and I will pay you" (Exodus 2:9b [NIV]).

Now, Pharaoh's daughter had no idea that this was Moses' mom. Moses' mom gladly took Moses and nursed him. When he grew older, she took him to the pharaoh's daughter, and he became her son. She named him Moses, meaning "drawn out of the water."

Moses' mom put God at the center of her plans. See how it panned out?

God was at the center of Moses' circumstances. God's plan was for Moses to be given to Pharaoh's daughter. His supremacy was clearly demonstrated.

How wonderful and mercy-filled of our heavenly Father to give Moses' mom the blessing to nurse her own son and save him from certain death in that decree of throwing Hebrew babies in the river. How long could a tar-lined basket hold a baby anyway? Only God could have saved Moses

An Adoption Story

This story makes me want to believe in God for the little things going on in my life right now. I call them little because, let's face it, in comparison to Moses', my problems seem insignificant.

For instance, God was there for me in the adoption of our son, Adam.

Adam came into our empty, barren lives through a series of events we did not seek or pursue.

It was the beginning of summer, and John and I were traveling to a northern state to find a home.

"Honey, where do you see us living? I mean, what kind of view would you like?"

"I would love to live near, or better yet, on a lake, Cindy."

"That would be fantastic. This is the land of lakes. Isn't it? We should be able to find something," I said.

After a long day searching for the perfect home, we arrived back at our hotel. I couldn't wait to get my tired shoes off and slip into my comfy sweats. By then, I was daydreaming of getting my feet up and cozying in the bed.

"What would you like for dinner?" John asked.

I couldn't care less. I was so exhausted. Normally I'd be smelling hot baked bread by this point or running to a restaurant with a nice white tablecloth. John noticed we had a message at our hotel. As I was changing into my end-of-day blessing clothes (as I affectionately call them after a hard day's work) John picked up the recording on our phone.

"Cindy, listen to this." The message was from an attorney who wanted us to return his call. John tentatively picked up the phone and began dialing. "What could it be, Cindy?"

A problem, of course. But what? we thought.

"Something with the sale of our home? Who knows?"

The attorney answered and got right to the point. "A baby has been born. Would you consider adopting him?

"What?"

"Someone is calling us to give us a baby. This is astonishing."

We had tried everything to have a baby, even fertility treatments. You name it, we tried it. At one point, we tried our hardest to find a baby to adopt, which turned out to be "a needle in a haystack," as we'd say to each other. It felt impossible. We gave up in the end, saying it wasn't God's plan. We were hopelessly devastated, though.

"How can this call be real?" I thought. We said "Yes, Yes, Yes," to the attorney.

That day, long ago, when the shocking, unexpected call came, it also just happened to be my birthday. It was and always will be the best birthday gift of my life. The attorney (now our attorney, Samuel) explained to us that the birth mom needed to decide who would raise her baby based off letters given to her from potential adoptive parents. We felt horrible for her having to make the most difficult decision of her life.

She chose us! Literally, weeks later, Adam was in our arms.

If God wants you to raise a baby, you will be raising one. Nothing can stop His plans from reaching completion (Job 42:2).

You can read a fuller version of our story in my aforementioned book *Tragedy Turned Upside Down*.

Just like Moses was raised by Pharaoh's daughter through quite a series of events, Adam became our child through quite a similar complicated series of events.

Behind it all, God's fatherly hands were orchestrating the scenes of His plans for each member of our family.

Who in a million years thought this could happen? I'm sure Moses' mom said the same thing. John and I are over the moon grateful for God's wonderful deeds in bringing Adam to us.

Adam grew in his birth mother's womb, and then, under God's divine plan, he was given to us to love, care for, and grow up into the terrific man he is today. Adam knows the story of his life well. We often quoted Psalm 139 to him.

He was knit together in his mother's womb ... all the days ordained for him were written in God's book before one of them came to be (Psalm 139:13, 16, my paraphrase [NIV]).

As solid as concrete, Adam, John, and I know this was God's plan for our lives.

From Murder to Midian

Moses grew up in the palace with Pharaoh, his daughter, and many servants. One day, while Moses was watching the Israelites, his very own people, he observed an Egyptian (from his adoptive heritage) beating a Hebrew. So Moses killed the Egyptian.

"No! Moses, what are you thinking?" I asked as I read this.

When Pharaoh found out about the murder, he sought to kill Moses. When Moses received this news, he fled to Midian.

I don't want to speculate, but it seems like there was not much regard for life or love in those days.

Moses met his wife in Midian and the couple raised a family.

Scripture says that Moses always felt like a foreigner in a foreign land. Imagine what Moses' life must have been like. He lived in a palace of Egyptians who disliked his people and saw them as outcasts (Exodus 2:15-22 [NIV]).

Then the pharaoh of Egypt died. Meanwhile, the Israelites were still slaves to the Egyptians and groaned against the harsh Egyptians. They cried out to the Lord and *"God looked on the Israelites and was concerned about them"* (Exodus 2:25 [NIV]).

The scene was being set. God was getting ready to call Moses into His work. Meanwhile, Moses was off leading a quiet life, tending his flocks in Midian.

Isn't that always when God calls us? When we're happily leading our quiet lives? God then revealed Himself to Moses in a burning bush, which is another famous passage. He spoke to Moses out of the bush, *"I am the God of your father"* (Exodus 3:6 [NIV]). Moses knew it was God Almighty.

When God wants to make Himself known to us, we can be sure He will do it.

The Lord conveyed to Moses that He was concerned about His people's suffering in slavery under the Egyptian's hands. He was coming to rescue them from the hand of the Egyptians and bring them out of that land into a good and spacious land flowing with milk and honey, the home of the Canaanites ... *"So now, go. I am sending you to Pharaoh to bring my people the Israelites out of Egypt"* (Exodus 3:10 [NIV]).

God's Call

I remember living a quiet life when God called me into leadership with Bible Study Fellowship (BSF), which is an international, inter-denominational Bible study.

I said to the leader at the time, "You must have read my information card incorrectly. I answered that I had little Bible knowledge when asked how well I know the Bible." That was thirty-three years ago.

Since then, I've led too many Bible studies to count, and I have had many opportunities to talk about our Jesus. I've written books about our great God. I've produced a program for Global 7.TV[31] called Treasures in the Storm, where I shared God's good hand in all our hard times, which were too many to count. All these opportunities were under the call of God.

Please understand that our abilities come only when God gives them to us. I call myself HIS container to bring His supremacy and glory to all He gives me. This is true for all of us.

Each of us are given a call from God, just like the call Moses was given at the burning bush.

Moses responded to God's command in Exodus 3:11 (NIV), *"Who am I that I should go to Pharaoh and bring the Israelites out of Egypt?"*

Oh, how we can relate to Moses' feelings of inadequacy. We get this, don't we?

Who am I to lead Bible study? What do I know? Our frail human-ness and inability in ourselves is overwhelmingly evident, isn't it?

I have many notes written by this next passage in my Bible. The notes say, "Look at how God comforts Moses."

Verse 12 states, *"I will be with you."* God even gave Moses a sign, *"'And this will be the sign to you that it is I who have sent you ...'"* (NIV).

There have been so many things God has called me to that I never felt equipped for. I felt I didn't know enough, I wasn't smart enough, or I wasn't talented enough.

Yet God always came through and accomplished His purpose in what He called me to do.

Moses and the elders went to Pharaoh. They were told by God to say: *"The Lord the God of the Hebrews has met with us. Let us take a three-day journey into the wilderness to offer sacrifices to the Lord our God"* (Exodus 3:18 [NIV]).

God knew Pharaoh would not let them go unless His mighty hand compelled him. So His mighty hand came in the form of plagues. After ten terrible plagues passed, God knew Pharaoh would let the Israelites go. This was the plan of God.

Moses was afraid the people would not believe his speech or believe what God had told him. So God gave Moses another sign for the people so that they would believe.

I'm so moved by God's merciful and gracious attitude toward Moses and his insecurities.

While writing my first book, I had much fear and trembling, but I knew God had called me to write it anyway.

My self-doubt and uncertainty ran off the charts.

Why would anyone read my book? That was my never-ending chant. I was a science major, not an English major.

Often, I inquired the Lord, "Are you sure, God?" I didn't have a writing bone in my body. On and on I presented worried questions to the Lord much like Moses did. Yet God was so gracious and patient with me, even in the times when I just wanted to give up. I even became sick to death of myself. I made myself miserable because of my lack of confidence.

Maybe you can relate. God gave Moses three miracles to perform in front of the people to show them He was involved.

I think if God gave me three miracles to perform, I'd be motivated and confident to write.

In Exodus 4, Moses objected to God's command, *"I have never been eloquent ... I am slow of speech and tongue."* The Lord responded, *"Who gave human beings their mouths? Who makes them deaf or mute? Who gives them sight or makes them blind? Is it not I, the Lord?"* (Exodus 4:10-11 [NIV]).

You are exactly who God intends you to be for the task He's called you to do.

Don't Miss Your Opportunity

We should highlight, underline, and write these scriptures on our foreheads. You are who you are because God made you that way, and by the way, it's perfect. How do you feel and how should you feel right now knowing you have been made perfect? You are perfect for being a wife, a mom, a friend, a daughter, a cousin, a sister, or a niece. The list is extensive and exhaustive.

I think of Nick Vujicic who was born with no arms or legs. He would not say he has birth defects or has a deficiency. He would tell you God made him that way. He'd tell you that he was made perfectly in God's sight.

Nick is an amazing man. These verses crystallize the truth of what Nick says to us. (Google him!)

Moses gave excuse after excuse as to why God should send someone else, as if God didn't know how to choose the perfect person for the job.

I hope this speaks to you as much as it does to me.

Finally, the Lord's anger burned against Moses (Exodus 4:14 [NIV]).

The Lord let him out of being the spokesperson and gave the job to his brother, Aaron (Exodus 4:14 [NIV]).

Lesson: Be careful when God asks you to do something that you feel especially unqualified for. Do it anyway! God will give you all things necessary to accomplish the task He's called you to do. You don't want to miss out.

We don't want God's anger to burn against us, do we? Or, more importantly, miss an opportunity to be blessed beyond belief.

Because those who had wanted to kill Moses were dead, he and his family returned to Egypt. The Lord commanded Moses, "*When you return to Egypt, see that you perform before Pharaoh all the wonders I have given you the power to do. When you go to Egypt perform the wonders I gave you the power to do for Pharaoh. But I will harden his heart so that he will not let the people go"* (Exodus 4:21 [NIV]).

The pharaoh refused again when asked by Moses and Aaron to let the people go worship their God. He said something along the lines of, "Why should I let them go? Who is this Lord anyway? Why should I obey Him? Get back to work. In fact, work harder with less supplies."

Ugh. Don't you just feel for Moses? Every time he tries to do what the Lord has asked of him, it ends poorly.

But also remember that the Lord hardened Pharaoh's heart. This was in God's preplans.

God Hardened the Heart of Pharaoh

God gives His reason for hardening Pharaoh's heart. Check out Exodus 10:1-2: *"Then the Lord said to Moses, 'Go to Pharaoh, for I have hardened his heart and the hearts of his officials so that I may perform these signs of mine among them that you may tell your children and grandchildren how I dealt harshly with the Egyptians and how I performed my signs among them, and that you may know that I am the Lord.'"*

It is of the utmost importance to God that we know He is supreme and that His character is perfect, holy, and full of righteous justice.

These horrible plagues we are about to look at were designed to show our children and our grandchildren Who the Lord is!

Also, God's purpose for hardening Pharaoh's heart was this. *"I will gain glory for myself through Pharaoh and all his army and the Egyptians will know that I am the Lord,"* (Exodus 14:4 [NIV]).

Again God said, *"I will gain glory through Pharaoh and all his army through his chariots and his horsemen. The Egyptians will know that I am the Lord when I gain glory through Pharaoh, his chariots and his horsemen"* (Exodus 14:17 [NIV]).

We see how God's design was to bring Himself glory through the plagues and the drowning of Pharaoh's men.

But before we get to the plagues and the parting of the Red Sea, we need to go back to Pharaoh's initial response to Moses.

We find out that what God commanded Moses to say actually got the Israelites into more trouble with Pharaoh and his officials, and it increased their harsh labor.

The Israelites told Moses, "*You have made us obnoxious to Pharaoh and his officials and have put a sword in their hand to kill us*" (Exodus 5:21 [NIV]).

Moses, frustrated, returned to the Lord. "*Why have you brought trouble on this people?*"... *you have not rescued your people at all*" (Exodus 5:22-23 [NIV]).

Discouraged, the Israelites refused to believe the latest word from the Lord. Even Moses felt hopeless.

Exodus 6:12 tells us, "*But Moses said to the Lord, 'If the Israelites will not listen to me, why would Pharaoh listen to me, since I speak with faltering lips?'*"

This seems like a logical point.

Yet we know the Lord's plans will never be thwarted. Remember our previous chapter?

Then Job answered the Lord and said, "*I know that You can do all things and that no purpose of Yours can be thwarted*" (Job 42:2). "*There is no wisdom, no insight, no plan that can succeed against the LORD*" (Proverbs 21:30).

This fact is edifying to our souls and comforting to our faltering minds. Oh, how I need this reminder in my repertoire of tools.

Speaking to Hardened Hearts

The Lord told Moses and Aaron to do as He commanded. "*Tell Pharaoh to let the Israelites go out of his country.*" But the Lord said, "*I will harden Pharaoh's heart, and though I multiply my signs and wonders in Egypt, he will not listen to you.*" Then the Lord said, "*I will lay my hand on Egypt and with mighty acts of judgment, I will bring out my divisions, my people, the Israelites*" (Exodus 7:2-4 [NIV]).

God has got a plan and we don't get to know what it is. Ever feel that way?

The Lord said He would bring out His people. That includes you and I. That's all we need to know.

I look back in my life at so many situations in which I couldn't see the plan, but later I was in awe of the mystery of God and His great provision.

We are not privy as to why the Lord does certain things. He does not have to give us this insight. However, God does show us His purpose for His people. It is hard for us to understand why the Lord told Moses to speak to Pharaoh when He (God) knew the Israelites were not yet going to be set free. But Exodus 7:5 gives the why. *"The Egyptians will know that I am the Lord when I stretch out my hand"* (Whose hand? God's hand) *"against Egypt and bring the Israelites out of it."*

God wanted the Egyptians to know He was the Lord. He was supreme. He had favor on the Israelites, His chosen people.

Now imagine if God tells you to speak to a people, let's say a group of women, but He tells you in advance, "I'm going to harden the hearer's hearts, and these women will not believe you or listen to you."

Ugh! How hard would that be? Maybe you have experienced that.

Years ago, I brought a marriage message to a church group under my husband's authority and under the authority of the pastor of the event. As I was speaking, men started getting up and leaving their seats. It was terribly distracting. I just reasoned that it was a much-needed bathroom break. The pastor got up, stopped my speech, and gave his congregation a scolding. The church's men were upset that a woman was speaking to them even when I was speaking only to the women in the audience under the pastor's authority.

Maybe this was similar to how Moses felt. I realized from Moses' example that all speaking is under God's divine authority; He must open peoples' ears if they are going to receive any message.

While the pastor was talking, I sat in the front row, looking out a large picture window in front of my seat. It was a spectacularly bright, crisp fall morning. A thousand bright yellow, red, purple, and green leaves lay on the ground. It was as beautiful as a Thomas Kinkade painting. A family of raccoons were played in the leaves. I wish I could have filmed their frolicking. I loved God's creation and all His fascinating animals. I was distracted and blessed all at the same time. God gave me a sweet show with His furry friends while these people hurtfully ignored my talk.

It's just like God to console us when we are undone by difficult circumstances.

Interestingly, the opposite is also true when God gives you an audience. He gives the hearers ears and hearts to believe the messages He's given you to speak. As the scripture says, how beautiful are the feet that bring the good news (Romans 10:15 [NIV]).

Suppose you have a difficult family member who is against you for something. This very tough conflict may be God purposefully working in your family to show a superior picture of love through resolve.

Our job is to keep ourselves postured in forgiveness and love even when people feel comparable to enemies. Sometimes we just cannot see God's plan yet.

1 Thessalonians 5:18 (NIV) tells us we are to *"give thanks in ALL circumstances; for this is God's will for [us] in Christ Jesus"* (emphasis mine).

Put God right in the center of it all.

The Ten Plagues

When Pharaoh didn't listen, the Lord began to do what He called "signs and wonders". Wonder means "something new, unusual, strange, great, extraordinary, or not well understood; something that arrests the attention by its novelty, grandeur or inexplicableness."[32]

The Lord told Moses that Pharaoh's heart would not give in and that he would not let the Israelites go.

In the morning, after he had come out of the river, Moses went to Pharaoh as the Lord had commanded him to do. God told Moses to confront Pharaoh on his disobedience. To tell him, *"The Lord ... has sent me to say to you"* (Exodus 7:16 [NIV]). After Moses struck the Nile, it turned into blood and the fish in it died and it stunk to high heaven. No one was able to drink its water.

"By this [Pharaoh] will know that I am the Lord."

Wow. Not what I'd want to do.

Why did the Lord do this? So that Pharaoh would know He was the Lord. The entire purpose was His supremacy.

The next plague involved frogs. Frogs invaded Pharaoh's bed and ovens. Everywhere the eye could see, there were frogs.

I live in Florida (not my native state) and every single evening I see nasty, huge, poisonous frogs. These are not cute gecko frogs; they are gigantic and scary. My neighbor called the other day and asked if John could help her get the varmints out of her pool.

The plague of frogs got Pharaoh's attention. In desperation, he asked Moses and Aaron to pray to God to take them away. Moses agreed, and the frogs died.

Yet again, Pharaoh hardened his heart and didn't believe in the Lord's power even after he received some relief. Maybe you've been tempted to act the same way as Pharaoh.

When the pressure is on me and I'm scared and suffering, I can make all kinds of promises to God. "Lord, I'll be so grateful if You heal me. I will tell everyone You have done it. I will pray more and spend more time with You. I will do everything You ask me to do. Lord, just please make me better."

But when the pressure is slightly lightened or when my burden is relieved it's amazing how I can relinquish my commitment. I justify how I don't need to take the next step in obedience like teaching or hosting a small group in my home, going on that mission trip when asked to help, visiting the homeless shelter when there's a need, hosting my family for the 4th of July, or bringing my mother-in-law to my home to live with me. After all, I convince myself that I am tired, I am busy, and I do a lot for the Lord already.

These are painful words to write.

God Has His Way of Getting Our Attention

Interestingly, God's next plague, gnats, could not be reproduced by Pharaoh's magicians. The magicians said to Pharaoh, *"This is the finger of God"* (Exodus 8:19 [NIV]).

God made Himself crystal clear to Pharaoh, but just as the Lord had said, Pharaoh would not have any of it.

God will see to every little detail. The magicians were getting a glimpse of discernment. They were starting to see Who the Lord God Almighty was.

Remember, the next time you're called to a God-sized project—the ones where you are disqualified or the ones that looks like a complete bust—remind yourself of God's work behind the scenes. He's doing everything necessary to complete the task that is already there.

God-Sized Projects

My impossible project was painting Sally's house.

I had a very special neighbor, Sally. Her sister was a believer in the Lord Jesus, and she wanted salvation for Sally. At the community pool one hot summer day, I ran into Sally's sister. I knew from across the pool deck it had to be her. I walked over to introduce myself. How do you do that, anyway?

Awkwardly I said, "Hello, my name is Cindy. Are you by chance Sally Smith's sister?"

"Yes, I am." We instantly bonded, just like young girls giggling over purple ice cream sprinkles.

Immediately we became kindred spirits and our number one bond was our love of Jesus.

Sally had been attending our Bible study the past year but was really struggling with believing God's word was literally true. Finally, one Tuesday after studying, she confessed and said she would not be coming back. My heart went dark and the wind sucked out of my sails. I was so vividly astonished. I hoped she didn't see my letdown. The last thing I wanted to do was bring more discouragement to her. I loved Sally. I so wanted her to know the worthiness of knowing Jesus. She was missing out on the best life has to offer in Jesus. He was the reason for my abundant life. I felt shattered to my core.

I prayed, "Lord, I let her down and you down, and what about her poor sister?"

Sally had put all her eggs in my Bible study basket. There was nothing I could say to change her mind. If I could, I would stand on my head and twirl for her to believe, but I couldn't make it happen. "God, please."

A few days later, I received a surprising text from Sally.

"Cindy, will you help me pick out paint colors for my living room?" Wow! Could this be my second chance?

"Yes, I would love to," I responded ASAP. I had a huge predicament. I was not qualified. I was not a decorator. Didn't we just read about that? I begged God to make me a designer. I didn't want to destroy her house.

After chatting with her, I offered to paint the room for her in a special faux style. She liked the finish in my home. What was I thinking? I got overzealous.

I wanted so much for her to like me so she'd like my Jesus that I offered to paint her living room. I'm not a decorator and I'm definitely not a painter. I reasoned to myself, *How hard can it be? It's just one room.* I was so far in by then that I couldn't see any way out.

Sally and I drove together to the paint store. It was a good connection as we shared our children's dramas. Jordan, her son, decided to feed the goldfish they won at the fair by dumping the entire container of food in the bowl. That trumped my son leaving his socks in our car for two weeks.

At the paint store, we agreed on two soft, sage tones to faux on the walls.

I literally winged it and begged God for favor. I thought, *I should stop by her house and see the living room a few days later.* Sally lived four doors from me, so Tuesday afternoon I walked down and rang the doorbell. She opened the door, which took my breath away. The living room was two stories tall. It was huge. Initially, I had no idea that this was the case. It was two weeks until Christmas. My plate was already spilling over with commitments. What a complete debacle I had gotten myself into!

I quickly left by saying, "Oh my gosh, I forgot …"

I went into a full-blown panic of the third degree as I left the scene. *What am I going to do? Confess I'm no decorator or painter?* All this was in the name of Jesus? "Lord, help."

Sally needed the room done ASAP because she was having a dinner party. All this was because of the very elaborate party she was having for Christmas.

I resorted to crying literal tears. After I settled down, I got a bright idea and called my best friend, Joan.

"Joan, you have to help me. Please. Help me paint this lady's house tomorrow." Being the best friend she was, Joan said she'd come but knew nothing about painting. I encouraged her by saying it was easy, and I'd show her how. That part was a fib.

Unfortunately, there wasn't a single moment for me to teach her how to faux paint before arriving at Sally's home.

My last-minute plan was to have her follow me with the rags of paint and do what I was doing. We prayed hard and the first miracle came. A man was at the house scaffolding in the living room and doing ceiling touch-up work. We could use his planks. I hadn't even thought about how to get up there during my sleepless nights of worry. Sally stayed to watch us paint for a while. Talk about adding misery to pressure. She eventually excused herself to run a few errands. I praised God!

Ready for the God's-got-it-already-done part?

The entire project took only four hours. It should have taken days. Sally came through the door mesmerized. She could not stop complimenting us on how beautiful it turned out. She said it was so much better than even her imagination had predicted. Joan and I left high as a kite on the miracle that had happened. We knew it! There was no way on God's green earth from inception to finale that we could have pulled that off without Him.

Joan and I asked God to remind Sally of His love every time she looked at her beautifully painted walls.

This was a God-sized project we were not qualified to complete. But God gave us everything necessary to complete the task. It was already done.

I don't know where Sally is today, but I do know God and His good purposes and how He answers our prayers. I'm 100 percent sure the task was fulfilled.

The Plagues Continued

Moses also had a God-sized project on his hands. It was underway with the Ten Plagues.

God's next plague of flies was different in that God sent them to the Egyptians but not to His chosen people, the Israelites. This was so everyone would know the distinction between HIS people and the Egyptians. God said, *"So then you will know that I, the Lord, am in this land"* (Exodus 8:22 [NIV]).

The Lord wanted to make it crystal clear to Pharaoh that He was present.

The flies covered all the houses and ground. Everything was ruined by the flies.

God will often send disasters so people know He is in the land. Could that be because it's the only way people will listen?

Isaiah 45:7 (NIV) says, *"I form the light and create darkness, I bring prosperity and create disaster; I, the Lord, do all these things."*

He is not a far-off God but the Father Who is nearby.

I heard a story from a pastor on God's good sovereignty.

It goes like this: A man gets in an accident and needs surgery. During the surgery, the surgeons discover he has cancer. With his cancer treated, he will have much greater longevity.

Surgery is bad and can physically hurt, but it can also heal us. Maybe in discovering that we need surgery, we'll unexpectedly heal a greater problem. It's like childbirth or heartbreak. Sometimes it's so painful but it's also so good for us. We need to look at things with our good God in the center.

It makes all the difference when we have put truth into our situations.

I experienced my own "surgery" experience with breast cancer.

In my book *Tragedy Turned Upside Down*, I share a story of my breast cancer and our son Adam's senior year of high school. I had been praying that he and I would have a wonderful last summer before college. Well, God brought breast cancer that summer.

"This, Lord, is how we have a great summer? Yuck!"

But as God only knew, it became the best summer ever. Adam never left my side. We had wonderful, deep, and abiding conversations every mom hopes to have. That year Adam gave me a Christmas present. It was a letter he wrote and framed. He embedded a picture of six foot him on my lap and wrote the letter around the picture. It was quite creative. In the picture, I was looking up at him and both of us were laughing. In his letter, he talked about how painful my breast cancer was for him to deal with but how God made everything ok and worked it out for a greater good.

Our family learned a lot about God's compassionate love, His care and unending comfort. He brought friends with the feet of Jesus to give us exactly what we didn't even know we needed. We were given wonderful homemade dinners like warm crusty bread (my favorite), creamy scalloped potatoes, marinated chicken in a stone-ground, honey mustard glaze, and for dessert, homemade flan.

I'd like to mention how much the personal touch in the meals meant to us.

I never knew until then. I was one of those people who used

my busy schedule to justify why I didn't have time to cook and I'd assume that Olive Garden or PF Changs would be better than my pasta. (By the way, you and I are never actually too busy for a God-sized project.)

How could I have been so wrong? Those meals made with so much love from my friends' hearts were some of the best, most comforting gifts our family ever received. Friends spent encouraging time with us and filled us with hope. They prayed for us and texted beautiful prayers. Others came to clean and bring groceries. There was nothing we lacked. It was truly the family of God. Only God could give that kind of love for us in our friends' hearts.

Questions to Consider during the "Surgery Seasons" in Your Friends' Lives

- Could God be tugging on your heart to be a blessing to someone who needs your help today?
- Could God be calling you to make a difference in your life today?
- Write out the outcome of your service to God from today.

2 Corinthians 9:6 reminds us, "*Whoever sows sparingly will also reap sparingly, and whoever sows generously will also reap generously.*"

God, in the Hardness of Our Lives

After the horrible fly infestation, Pharaoh asked Moses and Aaron to sacrifice to their God in Egypt. He was getting desperate but still would not let God's people leave Egypt. Moses refused his request because he had to go out of the land to sacrifice. Pharaoh finally agreed, "*but you must not go very far. Now pray for me*" (Exodus 8:28 [NIV]). However, Moses had heard this before from Pharaoh and he had reneged later.

So Moses essentially said, "Do not go back on your word again."

Well, can you see the writing on the wall? Yes, you guessed it, Pharaoh went back on his promise just as the Lord said he would.

The Lord was moving this king's heart like a water course.

Proverbs 21:1 (NIV) says, *"In the Lord's hand, the king's heart is like a stream of water that he channels toward all who please him."*

Remind yourself of this when your personal objections feel like mountains to be moved.

In Exodus chapter 9, verses 14-16 (NIV), the Lord declared, *"This time I will send the full force of my plagues against you and against your officials and your people so that you may know that there is no one like me in all the earth."* The Lord then said something so true about Himself. It was something I myself have been wondering. *"By now I could have stretched out my hand and struck you and your people with a plague that would have wiped you off the earth."* The Lord could have easily done that, but He didn't. Why didn't He? Verse 16, *"But I have raised you up for this very purpose ... that my name might be proclaimed in all the earth."*

I wonder about today's world affairs and the pandemic we just went through. Maybe God wants to proclaim His name to all the earth as He did to the Egyptians. We cannot even begin to understand God's plans. Only if He chooses to reveal them will we know them.

To all those who lost loved ones, my heart grieves for you. My husband spent ten very difficult days in the hospital, and I feared the worst.

I also think of two scriptures, one in Isaiah, where the Lord talks about how He is sparing someone from a greater evil when He takes them home.

Isaiah 57:1b (NIV): *"... no one understands that the righteous are taken away to be spared from evil."*

This is another passage on how God can't wait to see us and have us home with Him. It's like a parent who wants to see their adult child when they live across the country, only better.

Psalm 116:15 (NIV): *"Precious in the sight of the LORD is the death of his faithful servants."*

How can we begin to understand the hardness of life, and yet trust the character of the One Who brings life and takes life?

Deuteronomy 32:39 (NIV) says, *"See now that I myself am he! There is no God besides me. I put to death and I bring to life, I have wounded and I will heal, and no one can deliver out of my hand."*

If you have endured much loss and pain, I grieve with you. I've buried a son. And recently, both of my parents. What has helped the most is believing the fact that Jesus was involved and how much He cared about them, more than I am able to.

It's hard, hard, hard! But there is supernatural comfort in the middle of it all.

Yesterday I heard heartbreaking news. A dear sister in Christ fell and it caused her to have a brain bleed that is going to take her life. My heart breaks for her husband of many years and her adult children. It happened so suddenly and she loves the Lord so much.

I want to share God's supernatural comfort with them all. Yet I am confident they already know of this comfort because many years ago their very talented high schooler suffered a terrible injury. While playing in an evening basketball game, he chased after a ball and literally ran into the wall and broke his neck. He is a quadriplegic now. That tragic night his dad was at work in Washington D.C. when his beautiful wife (in a coma now) called to tell him the news. His response was, "God is good all the time." That's how I know they know.

My prayer is this. "God of all comfort, surround that family as only You can. Faith-filled Father, send your ministering angels."

Born for Justice

God rebuked Pharaoh in Exodus 9:17 (NIV), *"You still set yourself against my people and will not let them go."*

So the Lord sent the worst hailstorm ever seen on the planet.

Have you ever been in a hailstorm or seen one on TV? It's very traumatic. This was a serious disturbance.

If you were in Egypt at the time and did not take shelter, you would die. While some believed what was about to happen and took shelter, others did not and they died.

Still, Pharaoh would not let the people go.

So "the Lord said to Moses, '*Go to Pharaoh, for I have hardened his heart and the hearts of his officials so that I may perform these signs of mine among them that you may tell your children and grandchildren how I dealt harshly with the Egyptians and how I performed my signs among them, and that you may know that I am the Lord*'" (Exodus 10:1-2 [NIV]).

What, Lord? You want our children and grandchildren to know that You deal harshly with evil people who oppress Your chosen ones, Your children? You want them to know the horrible things You plagued Egypt with so that all would know You are the sovereign King of the Universe, a just and righteous Judge Who knows the future and what is best, Who does no wrong?

That's what You want them to know, Lord?

Strangely this is such a comfort. We have been born for justice; it's in our bones. We have been born to desire to know the immense character and profound bigness of our God. God is always revealing who He is throughout scripture.

I heard a message this weekend by a great pastor on 1 Kings 20:13.

"*This is what the Lord says*: '*Do you see this vast army? I will give it into your hand today, and then you will know that I am the Lord*'" (1 Kings 20:13 [NIV]).

What, Lord? The goal of God giving a vast army into the king's hands was so that they would know He was the Lord.

Also check out what 1 Kings 20:28 has to say: "The man of God came up and told the king of Israel, '*This is what the LORD says*: "*Because the Arameans think the LORD is a god of the hills and not a god of the valleys, I will deliver this vast army into your hands, and you will know that I am the LORD.*"'"

Again, the Lord will do what is necessary to reveal and make known His supreme, commanding dominance over all. He desires us to know how great He is!

It makes me think, *Many folks today talk about You, Lord, as squishy, soft, warm, cuddly, and a God Who does only kind, benevolent deeds. In truth, You are so exponentially above and beyond those words. You are a mighty, powerful King. The Ruler of all the universes. You hold all things in Your capable, trustworthy hands. All Your plans come to be.*

Psalm 33:9-11 (NIV) says, *"For he spoke and it came to be, he commanded and it stood firm. The lord foils the plans of the nations, he thwarts the purposes of the peoples. But the plans of the Lord stand firm forever, the purposes of his heart through all generations."*

Preparing for the Last Plague

The Lord said, *"I will bring one more plague on Pharaoh and on Egypt. After that, he will let you go from here, and when he does, he will drive you out completely"* (Exodus 11:1 [NIV]).

Interestingly, the Lord made the Israelites favorable in the eyes of the Egyptians, even Moses himself was highly regarded by Pharaoh's officials.

We should take note here that when God calls you to do a thing, He will give favor to you in the eyes of those you deal with; He will provide what's needed.

As we quoted from Proverbs 21:1 (NIV) earlier, *"In the Lord's hand the king's heart is like a stream of water that he channels toward all who please him."*

What could God be calling you to now, for which you need His favor? Write it down and do it.

Matthew 10:19 (NIV) says, *"But when they arrest you, do not worry about what to say or how to say it."*

How's that for a tremendous promise?

I'm reminded of a story from a dear friend. She was on the board of a university and wanted creation to be taught along with evolution at the college. Shaking in her boots, she went before the powers of being and presented her case. And yes, God went before my friend and gave her favor in the board's eyes along with the intelligence needed to present her case so that they would agree with teaching creation along with evolution. It was simply amazing.

That's how God's favor works. He plants us throughout history exactly where He wants us (Acts 17:26) and then performs His amazing, incomprehensible work through us just because He has decided to. When He uses us in this way, we are undone because we know the task's impossibility.

Where has God called you to be His container? He will work through you.

The Last Plague

The Lord instructed Moses to tell the Israelites to ask their neighbors for articles of silver and gold. This is the kind of favor from God that I talked about earlier.

Who, when asked, will give over all their silver and gold to the enemy? The Lord then asked Moses to explain that at midnight HE (God) would go throughout Egypt and kill every firstborn son along with every first-born cattle. But among the Israelites, not even a dog would bark because of the Lord's protection. *"Then you will know that the Lord makes a distinction between Egypt and Israel"* (Exodus 11:7 [NIV]).

We don't have to understand or critique what we have been told by God.

This was how it was going to unfold. The Lord was going to pass through Egypt and strike down every firstborn of Egypt, both people and animals. *"I will bring judgment on all the gods of Egypt. I am the Lord"* (Exodus 12:12b [NIV]). But the Israelites would be spared by smearing the blood of lambs over their doorposts.

This would become a lasting ordinance, a festival to the Lord to remind the people for generations to come of what the Lord had done and how He spared all the Israelites and delivered them from the hand of Pharaoh.

The Lord desires His chosen ones and all the earth to comprehend and grasp that He is the center of the universe. All of everything revolves around Him alone. He wants all creation to know His incomprehensible wisdom, love, care, and knowledge. His preference is for His people (Exodus 12:26).

Our Takeaway: You are held secure in your heavenly Father's arms though everything around may shatter. Chaos may engulf you, but be courageous. You are His chosen one and He is watching you. He is working for your best.

Take a moment to think about that.

What do you need God to be in the center of today? Where do you need Him to deliver you from the jaws of distress?

Job 36:15-16 (NIV) says, *"But those who suffer he delivers in their suffering; he speaks to them in their affliction. He is wooing you from the jaws of distress to a spacious place free from restriction, to the comfort of your table laden with choice food."*

So Many Whys

Little did I know…

Pam approached me on our walk. Being a dear, long-time friend, she challenged me to memorize the above Job passage with her. In the heat of our Indiana summer, I began to soak in the words.

God speaks to me in my suffering and in my affliction.

I thought to myself, *What suffering, what affliction? Things are really good right now. I'm enjoying the fruit of summer. There are literally fresh strawberries, peach pie, sunshine, blue skies, and no to-dos. Life is really great.*

Yet it was Pam who had asked me to memorize this passage, and I could never say no to her. Her vibrant love of Jesus was way too infectious to ignore. Little did I know how much I would need those two short verses for the rest of my life.

Why is it that we take such things as memorizing bible verses so flippantly? There happens to be a feeding of the soul of the highest kind in memorization. I never knew until I experienced this for myself.

I now appreciate the supernatural happenings as I engage in that detailed parsing when memorizing.

Shortly after I learned this passage and soaked it into my hungry soul, John told me that a dear friend, Neil, had just been diagnosed with a life-threatening cancer.

Neil was too young for this conclusion. His tribe of kids could fill a soccer team. Our hearts broke thinking about their dark storm. We met Neil's family at the hospital. He had already been checked in and was undergoing tests. It turned out we were the only ones there. Why that often happens is beyond me. That hospital room should have been bursting at the seams with friends and family of those two.

We burst into tears, blubbering unintelligible sounds as we hugged and comforted in platitudes. "It will be okay." As we shared our torn-apart hearts, that memorized scripture came in like a flood and I received the nourishment I needed. As I shared the verse with the family, I realized it was the perfect nourishment for their anxious and frightened souls too. This was the reason for my memorization.

Thank you, God. How often do we do things like this to only later see so many of the whys?

After the Plagues

The day came and Israel was let go; it was about 600,000 men, women, and children on foot.

God provided a pillar of fire by night to guide them to the promised land and a cloud by day.

Imagine all these people and farm animals being led by Moses, the boy from the tar basket.

The Lord moved Pharaoh's heart to want the Israelites back in his slave camps. He mused, "We lost our labor force." So he pursued the Israelites. As the Egyptians caught up, the Israelites looked back and trembled in fear saying, "We'd be better off staying in Egypt. Now we will die out here in the desert." Moses encouraged the people, "*Do not be afraid. Stand firm, and you will see the deliverance the*

Lord will bring you today. The Egyptians you see today you will never see again. The Lord will fight for you. You need only be still." (Exodus 14:13-14 [NIV]).

Who needs to hear that word today?

Do not be afraid in your hard circumstances! Stand firm! "*The Lord will fight for you. You need only be still*" (Vs. 14, NIV).

God is a Promise Keeper and Deliverer for all His people. I hope you, dear readers, are greatly encouraged. The Lord will fight your battles.

Just recently, I received a prayer request about a sweet young woman, Mary, who is pregnant and caught Covid. Her job asked her to get a vaccine but she is very afraid to do so for her baby's sake because she has heard many horror stories.

She needed to hear that the Lord was with her and that He would direct her path. He would pave her way. "*Trust in the Lord with all of your heart ... he will make your paths straight*" (Proverbs 3:5-6 [NIV]).

God moves king's hearts. He is not just the God of Bible characters. He's the living God of our very bodies and souls and the One Who is tenderly caring for this young mom. Although He alone knows His plans, we know His plans are good.

The Parting of the Red Sea

Luke 12:32 (NIV) says, "*Do not be afraid, little flock, for your Father has been pleased to give you the kingdom.*"

It is the Father's great happiness and good pleasure to give you the kingdom.

God "*works out everything in conformity with the purpose of his will*" (Ephesians 1:11 [NIV]).

Whatever you may be going through right now, God can be trusted with it. So let's bow our heads, stand tall, and watch Him work the wonderful deeds He is about to perform (Psalm 71).

We can imagine Moses and the Israelites were "going through it" at the foot of the Red Sea. The Lord commanded Moses to "*raise your staff and stretch out your hand over the sea so that the Israelites can go through the Red Sea on DRY ground. I will harden the hearts of the Egyptians so that they will go in after them ... The Egyptians will know that I am the Lord when I gain glory through Pharaoh, his chariots and his horsemen"* (Exodus 14:16-18 [NIV]).

Here are some interesting facts on the width and the depth of the Red Sea.

The Red Sea separates the coasts of Egypt, Sudan, and Eritrea to the west from those of Saudi Arabia and Yemen to the east. Its maximum width is 190 miles, its greatest depth is 9,974 feet (3,040 meters), and its area is approximately 174,000 square miles (450,000 square km).[33]

The Lord had Moses stretch out his hand over the sea so that its waters flowed over the Egyptians. Not one of them survived. The Israelites saw all the dead Egyptians and knew God had saved the Israelite people, and all who saw put their trust in the Lord.

Trusting God was the point back then and it's still the point today.

The Israelites were terrified and scared to death over the Egyptians chasing them into the Red Sea. If we were in their place, would we consider asking God to part the sea? No. Not a minuscule bone in our bodies would do that.

We are reading about God's incredible miracles. Maybe we should think outside of our box for a minute and simply believe HIM and trust His ways.

My Red Sea Story

I shared with a friend today about a house my husband and I bought years ago. It wasn't the first house we wrote an offer on; it was our third. We were on vacation when we wrote an offer on the first one, and someone else snatched it. "God has a different house," we said.

The second house was beautiful and in perfect condition. We waited to have our son, Adam, see it after school. We wanted him in the house-buying process because he was getting older. He was maybe 11 years old at the time. We arrived at the house and walked down the newly carpeted steps to the immaculately finished basement, only to step into three inches of water! We declined to write on that one. A close friend found the third house. Thank you, Deb.

The house needed work, but it was in the perfect location with a small, thick, very manageable wood behind it. I loved the privacy. With new paint, new wood floors, new countertops, and new appliances, it would be fabulous.

We wrote an offer. A church acquaintance recommended a home inspector. We closed and began the remodeling process. We found out later that it had sloping floors, bad windows, and it also needed a roof. Our inspector had missed all of these things. He was highly recommended too.

Our original plan was to have every upgrade done before we moved in, but God had other plans. John and I spent more hours than we could count encouraging workers who came to our home. The inspector sat at our kitchen table and sobbed as he apologized.

"We would have bought the house anyway," we said. Then a Grizzly Adams guy sat at our table and wept over his wayward children. Next, the tile man sobbed over his wayward wife. John and I felt like the Christian version of Dr. Phil.

Truth be known, our hearts are for the downtrodden. We are so grateful when we can bring hope to others. It's truly our life calling, sometimes to a fault.

Meanwhile, our floor was sinking into the crawl space. Another church friend and his son came over to look at the trouble.

He ended up jacking the house up and holding it in position with large, industrial jacks. It was a superb solution to a major problem. The jacks are probably still there today.

We call this house our best house of all.

We moved there in October, and I remember sitting outside and listening to a bell a neighbor had outside. This bell faintly rang with the slightest breeze. It reminded me of the foghorn I heard growing up near Lake Michigan. It was such a pleasant memory.

You see, this wreck of a house ended up being a complete treasure to our family.

God used us to encourage those struggling workers while blessing our socks off. We just needed patience and belief that He was in it all. We had to put Him in the center of the mess. If we had put us in the center, we would have been frustrated and miserable. *How come they didn't come yesterday? Why do I have to live with sub-flooring for eight months? I'm so tired of living with workers in my house. It costs so much more than they promised.* Get my point?

We had put God in the center. *They're not here today,* I'd remind myself.

God had the best timing for the house and all its projects. His purpose and persons and materials were all in His capable hands. With God in the center, our perspectives, our peace, and our happiness shifted in a positive direction.

Did the Red Sea part for us? We sold that house for much more than we paid, with the jacked-up foundation and all. It turned out that a builder bought it. He said it was not a problem.

Don't you just love how the Lord works?

I Want a Life Like That

When I think about God holding us in His hands, it reminds me of my flight to Florida.

John and I were sitting beside a sweet older man on one of our vacation flights to Florida. He was the happiest guy ever. He cracked silly jokes with the flight attendants and with everyone who passed by him. We were in the second row.

We learned his wife had passed away, and of course she had because the man was as old as dirt. Yet, he didn't have a care in the world. I bent over and asked him what his secret was to live such a happy life. He said God had always taken care of him and he had always been given what he needed; it was as simple as that.

The flight attendants fussed over him like he was the President of the United States. "Mr. Jones, would you like some more coffee?" "Can I get you a fresh glass of water?"

What a blessed man! He said every detail of his life was in God's hands. He really did not seem to have a care in the world.

And yet the man had problems. He needed a wheelchair to get around. Just imagine the loss of control you would feel if you needed someone to move you from point A to point B.

He also lived in his older 4-bedroom home and had children; some of them were married with kids. I could write a whole book on kids and grandkids' worries.

But truly I tell you, this man did not carry any of those burdens on himself.

I want a life where I do not have a care in the world!

Let's spur one another on just as this very old man spurred on John and me.

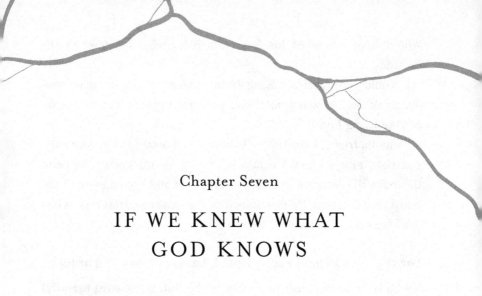

Chapter Seven

IF WE KNEW WHAT
GOD KNOWS

If we knew what God knows, we'd do the same thing exactly the same way.

I would have pulled Jonah off that boat to Tarshish. I wouldn't have let those sailors throw him to his likely death. I would have given him an umbrella of shade as he sat outside that sweltering city. But that would have stolen Jonah's repentance which came through his hardships, not to mention the entire city of Nineveh's salvation through his preaching.

Similarly,

"I would have pulled Joseph out. Out of that pit. Out of that prison. Out of that pain. This would have cheated nations out of the one God would use to deliver them from famine."[34]

I would have pulled Job out of his undeserved tragedy only to have all of us miss out on God's good supreme plan. Things Job said were too wonderful for him to know (Job 42:3b [NIV]).

I would have pulled Moses out of that tar-covered basket. I would have given him back to his mom. This would have kept the chosen people of Israel from deliverance and from seeing the one true God. It would have stolen God's glory.

I would have spared Paul from that blinding lightning bolt, which would have prevented his feet from bringing good news to the Gentiles.

I would have grabbed King Nebuchadnezzar out of that dew-drenched field, which would have prevented him from ever knowing the living Lord!

"And oh, friend. I want to pull you out ... I want to stop your pain. But right now I know I would be wrong. [God] knows the good this pain will produce."[35] He's watching you and keeping you in the midst of this storm. He promises that you can trust Him even when it all feels like too much to bear.

For the Days I Don't Know How I Am Going to Get Through

God is behind the scenes in my life, orchestrating the most beautiful work of art I've yet to see. He's supersonically catapulting me to His highest spot, the place where delight reigns free. I can't see a thing right now. My tunnel is black as night, pitch black. My emotions tell me to run, but I'm in a fiery free fall too paralyzed to dash. I want to crawl into a ball and hide from the world's turning.

"How, God, is this of any profit?" Yet there He is offering a warm, soft snuggly. If only I could grab hold of it. Oh, to sit in His heavenly surroundings for a few precious moments and be in a place where my skin is soothed. Maybe I would feel a bit whole just for a while. It's all waiting for me. God's calling me to come. It's all my choice. But will I choose to believe? Will I choose to get in His heavenly stroller?

Hope defined: Knowing our God rules and reigns right in the middle of all our footings. He stands triumphantly, rock solid, on the highest mount. Hold tight for the adventure of a lifetime. We're gaining hope like scaling Mount Everest.

God places a medal of victory around your neck and a trophy in your hand and says, "Child, it is already done."

He came to earth to be exceedingly more than we could imagine. He came to surpass all our expectations. He came to bind our broken hearts and literally set our bones back into place. He came to free us from captivity by ripping off shackles of despair and misery from our crusted body of unbelief. He came to bring us to a spacious table laden with our choicest foods (Job 36:16).

He came to release us from darkness and from all the blackened places where shining has ceased.

He came to proclaim the good news of great victory and bring a soothing balm, an oil of Gilead, for any open wounds, any lacerated body parts, and any decaying of the soul.

He came to make known to us the path of exuberant living, the place where He fills us with joyful pleasures in His presence (Psalm 16:11, my paraphrase).

When we treasure what we have learned into our hearts, we can be reassured in treacherous times. We can lift our eyes to where the buoyancy of our assurance lies.

This is the place where we have a glad-hearted expectation of something good that is coming. We don't yet possess it. We can't hope for what we already have, right? It's far too easy to be distracted by the cares and anxieties of this world. Our muscle memory is designed to look to the future with fear rather than with faith. There is a place where we need to roll up the sleeves of our minds, get clear and steady, and set our hope fully on the grace that will be brought to us. This place is where we need to set our hope fully on the tidal wave of coming grace. It is coming.

Oh, how necessary it is for us to drink deeply from this fountain.

The Real Truth

I cannot be expected to hide my opinions as an author when I believe them to be biblical, relevant, hopeful, and soul satisfying to you as the reader.

So here's my best shot on God's sovereignty and our responsibility.

Imagine you got up this morning excited about your plans for a productive day of house cleaning. You begin vacuuming all those crumbs from last night's football party. You dust under the couches grabbing Fifi's hairballs. You plan to then scrub the floors squeaky clean and have a delightful daydream of how spic and span your house is going to feel. You can smell the squeaky clean already. Lemon Verbena is delighting your spa mojo.

But then the phone rings and it's your neighbor. She tells you her husband has just been rushed to the hospital. You wonder to yourself, *How come I didn't hear the ambulance? Our houses are only twelve feet apart.*

You hang up, quickly get dressed, and you don't even think about how you look because a life is at stake. You rush over to your distraught neighbor and end up spending most of the day caring for her and her suffering family.

God's sovereignty was working behind your scenes all day, planning His good purpose for all those circumstances and all those people's lives. You made your plans early that morning but it was the Lord who directed your steps (Proverbs 16:9). Every one of your steps were ordained for you by God and were already written in HIS book before You were even born (Psalm 139:16).

I believe God's sovereignty is involved in every decision I make. There is an umbrella of Him over me. His plans trump my plans.

Every conversation said, every morsel chewed, every thought in my care, were all in His supremely capable hands.

The fall of a single sparrow. *"Are not two sparrows sold for a penny? Yet not one of them will fall to the ground outside your Father's care"* (Matthew 10:29 [NIV]).

The rolling of dice. *"The lot is cast into the lap, but its every decision is from the Lord"* (Proverbs 16:33 [NIV]).

The decisions of kings. *"In the Lord's hand the king's heart is like a stream of water that he channels toward all who please him"* (Proverbs 21:1 [NIV]).

The failing of sight. *"The Lord said to him, 'Who gave human beings their mouths? Who makes them deaf or mute? Who gives them sight or makes them blind? Is it not I, the Lord?'"* (Exodus 4:11 [NIV]).

The loss and gain of money. *"The Lord sends poverty and wealth; he humbles and he exalts"* (1 Samuel 2:7 [NIV]).

The suffering of saints. *"So then, those who suffer according to God's will should commit themselves to their faithful Creator and continue to do good"* (1 Peter 4:19 [NIV]).

"Lord, this one is hard. I will preach the truth to myself. I know you have a good plan. I know I can't see it. I will trust you in the hard."

The completion of travel plans. *"Instead, you ought to say, 'If it is the Lord's will, we will live and do this or that'"* (James 4:15 [NIV]).

The discipline of His children. *"'My son, do not make light of the Lord's discipline, and do not lose heart when he rebukes you, because the Lord disciplines the one he loves, and he chastens everyone he accepts as his son. Endure hardship as discipline; God is treating you as his children. For what children are not disciplined by their father?"* (Hebrews 12:5b-7 [NIV]).

Everything is laid bare before the Lord. *"For the word of God is alive and active. Sharper than any double-edged sword, it penetrates even to dividing soul and spirit, joints and marrow; it judges the thoughts and attitudes of the heart. Nothing in all creation is hidden from God's sight. Everything is uncovered and laid bare before the eyes of him to whom we must give account"* (Hebrews 4:12-13 [NIV]).

He gives repentance to souls. *"Opponents must be gently instructed, in the hope that God will grant them repentance leading to a knowledge of the truth"* (2 Timothy 2:25 [NIV]).

He gives the gift of faith. *"For it has been granted to you on behalf of Christ not only to believe in him, but also to suffer for him"* (Philippians 1:29 [NIV]).

He gives life and brings death. *"The Lord brings death and makes alive; he brings down to the grave and raises up"* (1 Samuel 2:6 [NIV]).

He crucified His Son. *"Indeed Herod and Pontius Pilate met together with the Gentiles and the people of Israel in this city to conspire against your holy servant Jesus, whom you anointed. They did what your power and will had decided beforehand should happen"* (Acts 4:27-28 [NIV]).

I'm learning how God used Jesus' horrible death. It covered our sins and showed us His incomprehensible love.

I've also learned about God's grace and mercy to us. Attributes I could not have known about Him any other way. Each attribute of God I could write a divinely wonderful book on.

As J.I. Packard shares in his book, *Evangelism and the Sovereignty of God,* there seems to be a contradiction in free will and God's sovereignty, an antinomy meaning "a contradiction between conclusions which seem equally logical, reasonable or necessary. An incompatibility between two apparent truths."[36]

"Each must be true on its own, but you don't see how they can be true together."[37]

Scripture teaches us that God controls all things, even our actions in accordance with His purposes.

Romans 9:20-21 (NIV): *"But who are you, a human being, to talk back to God? 'Shall what is formed say to the one who formed it, "Why did you make me like this?"' Does not the potter have the right to make out of the same lump of clay some pottery for special purposes and some for common use?"*

Ephesians 1:11 (NIV): *"In him we were also chosen, having been predestined according to the plan of him who works out everything in conformity with the purpose of his will."*

Proverbs 16:9 (NIV): *"In their hearts humans plan their course, but the Lord establishes their steps."*

We are also taught that we are responsible for our actions.

Romans 2:6-8 (NIV): *"God 'will repay each person according to what they have done.' To those who by persistence in doing good seek glory, honor and immortality, he will give eternal life. But for those who are self-seeking and who reject the truth and follow evil, there will be wrath and anger."*

John 3 tells us if we reject the good news, we are guilty of unbelief.

We are responsible and God controls it all. Although our minds can't get around it, those two truths must be held together side by side.

As Paul said in Romans 9:19 (NIV), *"Then why does God still blame us? For who is able to resist his will?"* How can God, who holds us responsible, condemn our actions when He's controlling them? This is a great question.

The scripture answers this in Romans 9:20-21 (NIV). *"But who are you, a human being, to talk back to God? 'Shall what is formed say to the one who formed it "Why did you make me like this?" Does not the potter have the right to make out of the same lump of clay some pottery for special purposes and some for common use?"*

When confronted with such undeniable facts, it's hard to believe we are in the hands of chance or trust in our ability to outmaneuver our situations.

It shows us that "The prayer of a Christian is not an attempt to force God's hand, but a humble acknowledgment of helplessness and dependence. When we are on our knees, we know that it is not we who control the world. It is not in our power, therefore, to supply our needs by our own independent efforts. Every good thing we desire for ourselves and others, must be sought from God, and will come, if it comes at all, as a gift from his hands."[38]

Yet if we choose to continue to deny what we have seen to be true, we will end up consumed in fear and mistrust of everyone. We will constantly look over our shoulders.

We know people who live in mistrust, waiting for the next shoe to drop, don't we? Let's vow to never be like them.

I am certain that all we have learned in these chapters will move us to the convincing truth of God's character and His supremacy, which He has displayed in His good sovereign love. His love has disposed Him to desire our everlasting welfare and He has the ability to secure it. These facts are fundamentally foundational for our security and happiness.

Let us be audacious, faith-filled men and women who believe the word and claim friendship with God. We do God more honor by coming boldly before His throne than hiding in self-conscious humility among the trees of the garden (AW Tozer paraphrase).[39]

Concluding Thoughts

God's sovereignty is relevant for children, adults, moms with breast cancer, and dying grandmas.

"For in him all things were created: things in heaven and on earth, visible and invisible, whether thrones or powers or rulers or authorities; all things have been created through him and for him" (Colossians 1:16 [NIV]).

Nothing can be outside of Him or His care, His concern, His compassion, and His love.

Zephaniah 3:17 tells us, *"The LORD, your God, is with you, the Mighty Warrior who saves. He will take great delight in you; in his love he will no longer rebuke you, but will rejoice over you with singing."*

And Charles Spurgeon said it best: "In light of all we have learned about God, let us put on our 'holiday attire and go forth to gather garlands of heavenly thoughts." All joy rests in the blessed Father. "Those cheeks ... crimsoned with red lines of blood from your thorn-crowned temple; such unbounded love cannot but charm my soul far more than 'pillars of perfume' ... the least glimpse of [Jesus' face] is exceedingly refreshing to my spiritual sense and yields a variety of delights ...

"He is to me my rose and my lily, my heartsease and my cluster of camphire.

"When he is with me it is May all the year round, and my soul goes forth to wash her happy face in the morning-dew of his grace, and to solace herself with the singing of the birds of his promises." [40]

Let us get to know Him as this all-encompassing treasure that He is.

"You make known to me the path of life; you will fill me with joy in your presence, with eternal pleasures at your right hand" (Psalm 16:11 [NIV]).

Oh, fellow travelers, do not leave the supernatural treasures you have accumulated through these pages without some written reminders for your soul's sake.

Until next time.

ENDNOTES

1 A. W. Tozer, *The Knowledge of the Holy: The Attributes of God. Their Meaning in the Christian Life,* 31935th ed. (San Francisco, Harper One, 2009), 92.

2 Ibid.

3 Charles Spurgeon, "Morning and Evening: The Classic Daily Devotional." (Uhrichsville, Barbour Books, 2018), https://spurgeonsmorningandevening.org/2023/08/27/morning-august-27th-2023/.

4 A. W. Tozer, *The Knowledge of the Holy: The Attributes of God. Their Meaning in the Christian Life,* 31935th ed. (San Francisco, Harper One, 2009), https://generositymonk.com/2016/10/27/a-w-tozer-the-goodness-of-god/.

5 Wikipedia. "Milky Way," Wikimedia Foundation, last modified August 15th, 2023, 00:55.

6 Ethan Slegel, "How Many Galaxies Are In the Universe," *Big Think* (blog), March 8th, 2022, https://bigthink.com/starts-with-a-bang/how-many-galaxies/#:~:text=The%20deepest%20image%20ever%20taken,limits%2C%20is%20capable%20of%20seeing.

7 Ray Ortlund, *Isaiah: God Saves Sinners.* Preaching the Word, (Wheaton, Crossway, 2012) 248.

8 John Piper, (Desiring God). "Everything exists, including evil, and is ordained by an infinitely wise and holy God to make the glory of Christ shine more brightly. Everything exists ..." YouTube, May 22, 2013. https://www.youtube.com/watch?v=WWb4PU_n1VQ.

9 Monergism by CPR Foundation, "Did God's Decree Bring About the Fall?", *Monergism* (blog), https://www.monergism.com/thethreshold/articles/onsite/decree_fall.html.

10 "Learn", Webster's Dictionary, Miriam Webster, updated August 12, 2023, https://www.merriam-webster.com/dictionary/learn.

11 Franklin Graham, *Rebel with a Cause.* (Nashville, Thomas Nelson Publishers, 1997).

12 Id., 120.

13 Franklin Graham, *Rebel with a Cause.* (Nashville, Thomas Nelson Publishers, 1997).

14 Ibid.

15 Ibid.

16 Alistair Begg, "Contentment," Truth for Life (website.) November, 2004.

17 Sarah Young, *Jesus Calling.* (Nashville, Thomas Nelson, 2004.)

18 "Thwart", Collins Online Dictionary, Collins, updated 2019, https://www.collinsdictionary.com/us/dictionary/english/thwart.

19 Charles Spurgeon, "Morning and Evening: The Classic Daily Devotional." (Uhrichsville, Barbour Books, 2018.)

20 Charles Spurgeon, "Morning and Evening: The Classic

Daily Devotional." (Uhrichsville, Barbour Books, 2018),
https://spurgeonsmorningandevening.org/2022/08/05/
morning-august-5th-2022/.

21   A. W. Tozer, *The Knowledge of the Holy: The Attributes of God.*
Their Meaning in the Christian Life, 31935th ed. (San Francisco,
Harper One, 2009.)

22   Charles Spurgeon, *The Metropolitan Tabernacle Pulpit, Vol.*
26: Sermons Preached and Revised. (London, Forgotten Books,
2018.) https://www.spurgeon.org/resource-library/sermons/
beloved-and-yet-afflicted/#flipbook/.

23   A. W. Tozer, *The Knowledge of the Holy: The Attributes of God.*
Their Meaning in the Christian Life, 31935th ed. (San Francisco,
Harper One, 2009.)

24   Spurgeon, Charles. "God's Providence." The Spurgeon
Archive. Midwestern Baptist Theological Seminary, Accessed
August 28, 2023. https://archive.spurgeon.org/sermons/3114.php.

25   Benson, Joseph. 1857. *Commentary of the Old and New*
Testaments. New York: T. Carlton and J. Porter. https://biblehub.
com/commentaries/benson/job/3.htm.

26   Spurgeon, Charles. "God's Providence." The Spurgeon
Archive. Midwestern Baptist Theological Seminary, Accessed
August 28, 2023. https://archive.spurgeon.org/sermons/3114.php.

27   Charles Spurgeon, "Morning and Evening: The Classic
Daily Devotional." (Uhrichsville, Barbour Books, 2018.)
https://spurgeonsmorningandevening.org/2023/08/17/
evening-august-17th-2023/.

28   A. W. Tozer, *The Knowledge of the Holy: The Attributes of*
God. Their Meaning in the Christian Life, 31935th ed. (San

Francisco, Harper One, 2009), 92. https://generositymonk.com/2016/10/27/a-w-tozer-the-goodness-of-god/.

29   Stewart, Don. 2011. *The Case for Christianity: A Cross Examination (The Jesus Series)*. Santa Ana: DYA Publishing. https://www.blueletterbible.org/Comm/stewart_don/the-case-for-christianity/10-the-resurrection-of-jesus-christ.cfm.

30   Charles Spurgeon, "Morning and Evening: The Classic Daily Devotional." (Uhrichsville, Barbour Books, 2018), https://spurgeonsmorningandevening.org/2023/06/16/morning-june-16th-2023/.

31   https://www.global7.tv/video-category/cindy-schmidler/.

32   "Wonder", Webster's Dictionary 1828, American Dictionary of the English Language, Noah Webster, Accessed Sept. 6th, 2023, https://webstersdictionary1828.com/Dictionary/wonder.

33   "How wide is the Red Sea where the Israelites crossed?" Tony — Antonakis Maritis, "Medium". January 30th, 2021.

34   Kimberly Henderson, "I Would Have Pulled Joseph Out...", Kimberly D. Henderson (blog), accessed September 9, 2023. https://kdhenderson.wordpress.com/i-would-have-pulled-joseph-out/.

35   Ibid.

36   J. I. Packer, *Evangelism and the Sovereignty of God* (Downers Grove, InerVarsity Press, 2008).

37   J. I. Packer, *Evangelism and the Sovereignty of God* (Downers Grove, InerVarsity Press, 2008). https://matthewzcapps.com/2014/11/11/40-quotes-from-j-i-packers-evangelism-and-the-sovereignty-of-god/.

38   J. I. Packer, *Evangelism and the Sovereignty of God* (Downers Grove, InterVarsity Press, 2008).

39   A. W. Tozer, *The Knowledge of the Holy: The Attributes of God. Their Meaning in the Christian Life.* (Cambridge: Lutterworth Press, 2022).

40   Charles Spurgeon, "Morning and Evening: The Classic Daily Devotional." (Uhrichsville, Barbour Books, 2018.) https://spurgeonsmorningandevening.org/2023/05/01/morning-may-1st-2023/.

ABOUT THE AUTHOR

 Cindy Schmidler is a Sunshine Peddler. Weariness Exterminator. Cancer survivor. Grateful wife and mother. She is also a speaker, life coach, and teacher. She is the author of *Tragedy Turned Upside Down* and *God Is In Your Mess.* To really connect with author Cindy Schmidler, just tune in to spend time with the author and her pet dog Willie on social media, where she shares encouragement for your life and spiritual fuel for your journey.